Colbert's and d'Astous's contribution to understanding consumer behaviour in an Arts and Culture context will be welcomed by arts administrators, arts marketing educators, and arts policy makers everywhere. Getting to the "new normal" will require, more than ever, the kind of in-depth comprehension of factors influencing consumer behaviour that the authors help us to understand.

—**Leighann C. Neilson, PhD**, *Associate Professor, Marketing, Sprott School of Business, Carleton University, Ottawa, Canada*

Consumer Behaviour and the Arts

Although the literature on marketing of the arts is abundant, very few (if any) full-length works have examined the other side of the coin and closely studied the people who consume the products of the cultural industry.

This book offers a summary of the knowledge garnered in recent decades by researchers exploring consumer behaviour in arts and culture. Each chapter explores a different aspect of consumer behaviour in the arts by answering the following questions:

- What do we know about this aspect of consumer behaviour in general?
- What do we know about this aspect as it relates to the consumption of art works or cultural experiences?
- What are the practical implications of this knowledge for managers working in the arts?
- What are the implications for researchers in this field?

This book fills the need for scientific and practical knowledge about the people who consume arts and culture and will therefore be of particular interest to managers of cultural venues and institutions, to students or teachers in arts management training programmes, to researchers in the field, to public policymakers in arts and culture, and to anyone directly or indirectly involved in creating, promoting, and distributing artistic and cultural products.

François Colbert is a professor in the Marketing Department at HEC Montréal and holds the Carmelle and Rémi-Marcoux Chair in Arts Management. He serves as a co-director of the MMIAM programme (Master of Management in International Arts Management).

Alain d'Astous, PhD, is an honorary professor and researcher associated with the Camille and Rémi-Marcoux Chair in Arts Management at HEC Montréal. He is a fellow of the Royal Society of Canada.

Discovering the Creative Industries
Series Editor: Ruth Rentschler

The creative and cultural industries account for a significant share of the global economy. Gaining and maintaining employment and work in this sector is a challenge and chances of success are enhanced by ongoing professional development.

This series provides a range of relatively short, student-centred books which blend industry and educational expertise with cultural sector practice. Books in the series provide applied introductions to the core elements of the creative industries. In sum, the series provides essential reading for those studying to enter the creative industries as well as those seeking to enhance their career via executive education.

Managing Organizations in the Creative Economy
Organizational Behaviour for the Cultural Sector
Paul Saintilan, David Schreiber

Strategic Analysis
A Creative and Cultural Industries Perspective
Jonathan Gander

The New Arts Entrepreneur
Navigating the Arts Ecologies
Gary Beckman

Consumer Behaviour and the Arts
A Marketing Perspective
François Colbert and Alain d'Astous

For more information about this series, please visit:
www.routledge.com/Discovering-the-Creative-Industries/book-series/DCI

Consumer Behaviour and the Arts

A Marketing Perspective

François Colbert and Alain d'Astous

LONDON AND NEW YORK

First published 2022
by Routledge
2 Park Square, Milton Park, Abingdon, Oxon OX14 4RN

and by Routledge
605 Third Avenue, New York, NY 10158

Routledge is an imprint of the Taylor & Francis Group, an informa business

© 2022 François Colbert and Alain d'Astous

The right of François Colbert and Alain d'Astous to be identified as authors of this work has been asserted by them in accordance with sections 77 and 78 of the Copyright, Designs and Patents Act 1988.

All rights reserved. No part of this book may be reprinted or reproduced or utilised in any form or by any electronic, mechanical, or other means, now known or hereafter invented, including photocopying and recording, or in any information storage or retrieval system, without permission in writing from the publishers.

Trademark notice: Product or corporate names may be trademarks or registered trademarks, and are used only for identification and explanation without intent to infringe.

British Library Cataloguing-in-Publication Data
A catalogue record for this book is available from the British Library

Library of Congress Cataloging-in-Publication Data
Names: Colbert, François, editor. | Astous, Alain d', 1952– editor.
Title: Consumer behaviour and the arts: a marketing perspective / edited by François Colbert and Alain D'Astous.
Description: 1 Edition. | New York, NY: Routledge, 2022. | Series: Discovering the creative industries | Includes bibliographical references and index.
Identifiers: LCCN 2021019146 (print) | LCCN 2021019147 (ebook)
Subjects: LCSH: Consumer behavior. | Arts—Marketing. | Marketing.
Classification: LCC HF5415.32 .C65426 2022 (print) | LCC HF5415.32 (ebook) | DDC 658.8/342—dc23
LC record available at https://lccn.loc.gov/2021019146
LC ebook record available at https://lccn.loc.gov/2021019147

ISBN: 978-0-367-20728-1 (hbk)
ISBN: 978-0-367-20730-4 (pbk)
ISBN: 978-0-429-26311-8 (ebk)

DOI: 10.4324/9780429263118

Typeset in Calvert
by codeMantra

Contents

List of figures — x

List of tables — xi

About the authors — xii

About the cover artist — xv

Preface — xvi

PART 1

Introduction — 1

Chapter 1 Introduction to cultural consumption — 3
- A night at the opera — 4
- The consumption of arts and culture — 7
- A conceptual model — 9
- Premises and chapter structure — 12
- References — 13

PART 2

The psyche — 15

Chapter 2 Personality and self-concept — 17
- Personality — 17
- Self-concept — 21
- Personality and self-concept in the field of arts and culture — 22
- Implications for the marketing of arts and culture — 26
- Implications for research — 27
- References — 28

PART 3

Experience   31

Chapter 3 Perception   33
Selective perception   *33*
Perceptual organization   *34*
Interpretation   *36*
Perception in the field of arts and culture   *38*
Implications for the marketing of arts and culture   *44*
Implications for research   *45*
References   *46*

Chapter 4 Learning   49
Consumers are learners by nature   *49*
Learning in the field of arts and culture   *58*
Implications for the marketing of arts and culture   *62*
Implications for research   *64*
References   *65*

Chapter 5 Attitudes and affective states   68
Consumers live affective experiences   *68*
Affective experiences in the field of arts and culture   *77*
Implications for the marketing of arts and culture   *81*
Implications for research   *82*
References   *84*

Chapter 6 Decision-making   87
The consumer decision process   *87*
Decision-making in the field of arts and culture   *93*
Implications for the marketing of arts and culture   *98*
Implications for research   *100*
References   *101*

PART 4

The social environment   103

Chapter 7 Reference groups, culture, and subcultures   105
Reference groups   *105*
Different types of reference group influence   *109*
Influencers   *110*

Culture	*112*
Subcultures	*114*
Reference groups, culture, and subcultures in the field of arts and culture	*115*
Implications for the marketing of arts and culture	*120*
Implications for research	*122*
References	*123*

PART 5

Conclusion 125

Chapter 8 Marketing culture and the arts	127
References	*130*
Appendix 1 Scientific journals and training programmes related to arts and culture (A&C) marketing	131
Index	135

Figures

1.1	A conceptual model for the consumption of arts and culture (A&C)	10
3.1	The perceptual cycle (from Neisser, 1976)	37
4.1	The classical conditioning process	50
4.2	An Information processing model to explain and describe mental processes (d'Astous et al., 2018)	53
4.3	A hypothetical associative memory network	54
5.1	The one-dimensional perspective (d'Astous et al., 2018)	69
6.1	A model of the consumer decision process	88
6.2	Principal types of decision processes (Colbert et al., 1993)	98

Tables

5.1	Two fictitious cognitive structures (attitude towards Cirque du Soleil)	71
5.2	The Richins typology of emotions	75
6.1	Position of three museums in relation to three selection criteria	90
7.1	The different types of influence exerted by reference groups	110
7.2	The position of five countries according to the cultural dimensions of Hofstede	114

About the authors

Professor François Colbert

Holder, Carmelle and Rémi-Marcoux Chair in Arts Management, HEC Montréal

François Colbert is among top scholars in arts marketing in the world, having published close to 200 works and being one of the most cited authors in his discipline. He founded the Master in the Management of Cultural Organizations (in French) at HEC Montréal in 1988. He currently is a coordinator of the joint Master of Management in International Arts Management (HEC, SMU, Bocconi), the head of the field Marketing and Management of Arts and Cultural Industries at the PhD programme, and the founding editor of the *International Journal of Arts Management*, published by the Chair in Arts Management. He has been UNESCO Chair in Cultural Management from 2012 to 2018.

In 2002 he was awarded the Order of Canada for his many achievements and for his unique contributions in developing the field of arts management, the Queen Elizabeth II Golden Jubilee Medal (2002), and the Queen Elizabeth II Diamond Jubilee Medal (2012). He was made fellow of the Royal Society of Canada in 2005 and also received the ACE Award 2006 from the Association of Cultural Executives as well as the World Outstanding Scholar Award of Creative Management in 2021 (Sichan University). He is also an honorary professor at Peking University, the National Academy of Chinese Theatre Arts, as well as at the Tianjin Conservatory of Music in China.

Professor Colbert has been active in the field of arts and culture for over 40 years, particularly in the performing arts, museum, and film sectors. He has given numerous training and professional development seminars in arts management, with a focus on the field of marketing management in a cultural context.

He is a past or present member of the board of directors of 30 cultural organizations and has served as the vice-chair of the Canada Council for the Arts for eight years, until 2003; he has been on the Board of other large organizations such as Les Grands ballets canadiens and Radio-Québec.

He teaches Arts Marketing and Cultural Brand and Product Management at the master level, and a doctoral seminar called Fundamentals of Arts Marketing. He is also the author of Le Marketing des arts et de la culture, now in its fifth edition and available in English as Marketing Culture and the Arts as well as in 13 other languages (15 in total). Professor Colbert is the founding president and co-chair of the scientific committee of the International Conference on Arts and Cultural Management (AIMAC).

François Colbert is the author of close to 200 publications including articles in refereed and non-refereed journals, books, chapters in books, proceedings, bibliographies, and research reports, mainly on marketing of the arts and his Google Scholar 2020 Citations is as follows: Citations 3,238, H Index 24, I10 Index 43.

In addition, he has organized numerous conferences addressing topics related to cultural management. He has also given many talks and seminars on arts management both in Quebec and Canada and in 29 other countries, including Australia, Belgium, China, Colombia, France, Germany, England, Italy, Japan, Russia, South Korea, Spain, Sweden, and Spain.

Alain d'Astous is an honorary professor and researcher associated with the Camille and Rémi-Marcoux Chair in Arts Management at HEC Montréal, Québec, Canada. He is the author or co-author of more than 100 marketing and consumer behaviour articles published in various North American, European, and Asian refereed journals. He has been a member of the Editorial board of several journals and is currently on the board of *International Marketing Review*, *Journal of Advertising*, *Journal of Consumer Policy*, and *Psychology & Marketing*. He has been an invited scholar in several universities around the world, including the École Supérieure des Sciences Économiques et

Commerciales (ESSEC, France), the Università Bocconi (Milan, Italy), the University of Canterbury (Christchurch, New-Zealand), the University of Technology Sydney (Australia), and the Université Paris-Dauphine (Paris, France). He is a fellow of the Royal Society of Canada.

About the cover artist

Jeannette Perreault lives in Montréal. Her works can be found at Galerie Valentin in Montréal, at the Roberts Gallery in Toronto, as well as at the Singulart Gallery in Paris. The artist started her career in 1986 after obtaining her major in drawing and history of Arts at the Université du Québec à Montréal. She also participated in several living models workshops. She is attracted, among other subjects, by the performing arts, and she often draws musicians, dancers, and actors while standing in the wings of the Théâtre du nouveau-monde in Montréal. She starts by making a sketch of the performers, then recreates the scene as an oil painting on canvas. Over the course of her career she did 25 solo exhibitions and many collective exhibitions. Her paintings are part of private collections in Canada, the United States, Europe, and Asia.

Website: jeannetteperreault.com

Preface

Arts and culture are an integral part of our lives. The music we listen to, the books we read, the television series we follow, the films we watch at home or in the cinema—these are just a few examples of the many artistic and cultural products we consume on a regular basis. These products exist because they satisfy our needs and desires, whether we seek to acquire knowledge or simply wish to be entertained. But while their existence has this basic, undeniable dimension of personal enrichment, it also has a highly significant economic dimension. For example, in a December 2015 report entitled "Cultural Times: The First Global Map of Cultural and Creative Industries", UNESCO estimated that cultural and creative industries generated $2,250 billion in worldwide revenues in 2013 and employed almost 30 million people. Given such numbers, we should not be surprised that organizational management in this sector has become, over time, a significant field of application and research.

As researchers in marketing, the authors of this book are convinced that a deep knowledge of the people who consume the products of the arts and culture sector is crucial for its economic vitality. Marketing is a management philosophy in which consumers hold a central position. According to this philosophy, an organization must plan and implement its marketing activities to satisfy the needs and desires of consumers while also meeting its profitability targets. Therefore, this book aims to present a synthesis of the knowledge accumulated by researchers not only in marketing but also in other fields such as psychology or sociology—on the behaviour of consumers in general and, more specifically, on how people consume artistic and cultural products.

We have written this book with several types of readers in mind. The primary target audience is the managers who work in organizations directly or indirectly linked to the arts and culture sector. We hope our synthesis of the knowledge and research developed over recent decades will enable them to make better management decisions. Second, this book is also relevant for anyone completing a training programme to pursue a career in arts administration. It should help them enhance their managerial skills by acquiring a theoretical and practical knowledge of arts and culture consumer behaviour. Third, the book will benefit anyone with an intellectual interest in this field of research—either because they contribute to it systematically, and therefore wish to identify themes to fuel their ideas and projects, or because they have a basic desire to learn more about it. The teachers of training programmes in arts administration and culture management represent another target audience since our text provides a base of practical and theoretical knowledge they can transmit to their students. Furthermore, we believe this book will interest the people who create and deliver the products and services that sustain the arts and culture sector—the artists, creative directors, and museum curators who prepare exhibitions; the performing arts centre managers who review artistic proposals and plan a season for their city's different target audiences; the festival directors and talent agents who organize large-scale events. Last, since public cultural policies are directed at the consumer citizen, this book should be useful for government officials who design financial aid programmes in support of cultural enterprises, as it will help them understand the behaviour of the citizens whose interests they serve.

François Colbert (francois.colbert@hec.ca)
Alain d'Astous (alain.dastous@hec.ca)

INTRODUCTION
PART 1

Introduction to cultural consumption

Chapter 1

As we write these lines, in December 2020, the planet is in the grips of a devastating pandemic that has killed nearly 1.7 million people. The effects of this pandemic are not limited to a global health crisis—they are ravaging multiple sectors of the economy. And, indisputably, we can identify the arts and culture (A&C) sector as one of the most heavily damaged. What happens to a theatre company when, overnight, it is forced to cancel its current season because indoor gatherings of more than ten people have been banned? What happens to cinemas, concert halls, museums, opera houses, and circus troops—to all those places and organizations we usually associate with A&C—when severe constraints are imposed on physical proximity? As anyone can surmise, a great many A&C companies and organizations are in the business of serving crowds at indoor or outdoor events which lack physical distancing (festivals, for example), or of serving individuals or small groups who circulate in closed environments (such as museums) with little room for people to remain apart.

So, what happens next? Companies and organizations adapt, as they always do. They use their ingenuity to devise strategies for keeping their clientele supplied with the desired products, even while they bend to the constraints imposed upon them. One symphony orchestra will choose to perform their repertoire to fewer spectators, while another will opt for

DOI: 10.4324/9780429263118-2

online programming, and yet another will design a mix of the two. A&C managers are no less creative than the products they market.

At the heart of any strategic management approach, whether it seeks to mitigate the effects of a pandemic or achieve other objectives (e.g., increasing traffic, attracting new audiences, surpassing competitors), is one essential component we must consider if we are to succeed: the consumer. The best business strategy is one that delivers the desired results, and those results will generally depend on how consumers react. A deep understanding of the consumer is also of the utmost importance for anyone involved in running an organization— whether it operates in A&C or another sector—because ultimately it is the consumer who decides the fate of the organization's strategies.

The purpose of this book is to present a synthesis of the knowledge accumulated in recent decades on the behaviour of A&C consumers. Cultural consumption represents a very active field of research and practice. For proof, we need to look at Appendix 1 of this book. It lists the various scientific journals that publish on topics directly or indirectly related to this field (see also Colbert, 2014, 2017; Colbert & Dantas, 2019; Colbert & St-James, 2014); the associations that are involved in promoting research and disseminating knowledge; and the study programmes that provide training to researchers and practitioners.

A NIGHT AT THE OPERA

To introduce the study of consumer behaviour in the A&C sector, we will use a fictional but true-to-life story about one consumer's experience with one cultural product: a night at the opera. The story involves a young Japanese student named Takumi Suzuki. He resides in Sydney, Australia, while pursuing a university degree in engineering. For the purposes of this example, let us suppose we can see what Takumi has written in his personal diary, shortly after attending a performance at the Sydney Opera House. As we learn in the entry below, it was an Australian friend named Frank who offered to take him. The evening turned out to be a very positive experience.

January 28, 2020

I have to admit it—when Frank offered to take me to a show at the opera house last week, I was puzzled. The opera? I don't know the first thing about it. And I generally steer clear of things I am not familiar with. I was quite reluctant at first, but Frank insisted so much that I ended up saying yes. He's a good friend so I decided it was okay. He was right to insist—and I am glad I said yes—because we had a great time! I would not have traded that evening for anything else in the world.

The day after agreeing to Frank's idea, I went to the Sydney Opera House website to learn a little more about the opera we would see, the Barber of Seville, written by an Italian composer named Gioachino Rossini (I know I spelt that right because I kept the program, LOL). I read a plot summary and the story seemed both simple and complicated, with lots of characters, intrigues, and twists. To get a feel for the music, I also listened to a few excerpts on YouTube. I admit that up until then I knew nothing about the opera, but some of the tunes I heard were familiar, especially the aria of Figaro (La . . . La La La La La La LA!).

It may sound childish, but I was worried about what clothes to wear. I asked Frank, and he told me not to stress about it—neat and casual clothes were good enough, just not our usual gear for the beach. Phew! For a while I thought we had to dress up formal, which is not my thing, really.

The performance was scheduled to start at 8 p.m., but Frank told me to arrive earlier so we could listen to a well-known musicologist talk about this opera. We made it to our seats at 7:00 p.m. on the dot, and then were treated, along with other opera fans, to a talk about the composer's life, the social background of the composition (the French Revolution, the class struggle), the type of opera . . . and I even learnt a new term in Italian: "opera buffa", which means a kind of comic opera. I'm sure I enjoyed the performance much more because I had this background information.

How can I describe my first experience at an opera house? As for the show itself, I loved the big stage set (a two-story house with raised floors for the characters to cross), the lively acting style, the way the songs rolled into each other (my favourite was Rosine's aria "Una voce poco fa"), the funny antics, the mesmerizing music . . . I never knew we could experience so many emotions in such a short period, during just one musical and theatrical performance.

But there's a lot more to it. I realized a night at the opera goes far beyond just listening to the music and the songs. The experience combines so many different elements: the welcome for spectators, the size of the amphitheatre, the comfort of the seats, the atmosphere, the acoustics, the refreshments during the intermission, and so on. Ultimately, even if a performance is not the best ever, the whole experience can be great when all these other elements reach a high standard.

I really fell in love with the Sydney Opera House, so I am planning to invite my friend Frank to go with me on a new operatic adventure. I have already begun to make notes about the upcoming shows. Could this be the start of a new passion?

This story provides an example of how a cultural product, in this case the opera, is consumed. We might choose other A&C products to illustrate the different activities that shape this type of consumer experience. Let us clarify what we mean by the field of A&C. For the purposes of this book, we have adopted the typology of Colbert et al. (2018), which views cultural enterprises broadly as encompassing the following types:

- Performing arts: Theatre, music, dance and opera;
- Heritage: Museums, exhibition centres, whether built or intangible;
- Cultural industries: Publishing, film, sound reproduction, crafts;
- Broadcast media: Radio, television, Internet.

This typology also covers all the stakeholders who produce, reproduce, distribute, or preserve the works which artists create and performers perform. Thus, the performing arts category also includes the producers (such as theatres and theatre companies) and the broadcasters, concert halls, and festivals. The same applies to cultural industries that reproduce original works in physical formats such as printed books, or in electronic formats on digital platforms (Netflix, Spotify, Amazon, and so on). We include, in this typology, the broadcast media which are both producers and distributors of content, and the museums and film libraries whose chief mission is to conserve heritage works for the benefit of present and future generations.

The particular background we chose for our story—the experience of consuming a cultural product after receiving an invitation from a friend—was no accident. A&C organizations use a range of promotional methods with their subscribers when seeking to expand their consumer base or maintain traffic at an acceptable level (Stuckey, 2020); these methods include "bring a friend" referral programmes which offer the invited person a discount on the entrance fee or subscription price. To our knowledge, the effectiveness of these programmes has not yet been examined in a thorough research study. As one can see above, we have nevertheless taken the liberty of inventing a story ending which would certainly appeal to the marketing director of the Sydney Opera House.

This example will introduce a number of the concepts we study in this book. We will also use it to develop a conceptual model for understanding A&C consumer behaviour—one that will serve as the foundation for our ideas in the different chapters.

THE CONSUMPTION OF ARTS AND CULTURE

For the purposes of this text, we define the "consumption of arts and culture" (or "cultural consumption") as the cognitive, emotional, and physical activities of consumers when they select, buy, consume, and dispose of goods and services related to arts and culture (A&C) in order to satisfy their needs and desires. Our definition also includes the factors which influence these activities.

Let us revisit Takumi's story, the fictional narrative presented above, and analyse it with the various elements of this definition in mind. During his "encounter" with the opera, Takumi engages in a range of activities. For example, he thinks about his friend Frank's invitation and wonders what the appropriate dress for the event should be (cognitive activities). He goes to the Sydney Opera House to attend a pre-concert lecture about the Barber of Seville, and then witnesses the performance itself (physical activities). He experiences several different emotions during the performance (emotional activities).

Such activities occur, to varying degrees, in most episodes where artistic or cultural products are consumed. Typically, four basic processes are involved: choosing, buying, consuming, and disposing. For example, after a reflection period, Takumi *chooses* to accept the invitation from his friend Frank. Then—although the story does not mention it—the opera tickets are *bought*. Takumi's *consuming* of the product was not only his attendance at the performance but also his use and enjoyment of everything connected with the event: the hall, the venue, the staff, the refreshments, and so on. Last, we note that Takumi kept his copy of the event programme; he does not *dispose* of it, because he may keep it as a souvenir.

Consumers engage in these activities and processes because they seek to satisfy their needs and desires. These needs and desires generally relate to the cultural product concerned, but they may also relate to other elements of the consumer situation. For example, does Takumi really have a desire to attend an opera? A desire to strengthen his friendship with Frank appears to be the real motivating factor instead. Clearly, we can link the needs and desires of cultural consumers with multiple elements that determine how they experience the consumption process. But to do so, we must distinguish needs and desires associated with more utilitarian (or functional) benefits from those associated with more hedonic (or intangible) benefits. For example, the act of *buying* opera tickets via the Internet has a mainly utilitarian motivation, whereas the act of *listening* to an opera is rooted in a desire to be entertained, to experience pleasure. Furthermore, it is important to note that the act of consuming A&C is often highly symbolic. Naturally, we attend an opera to have a good time and appreciate the music, the arias, the set design, the plot of the story, and so on. But being an opera lover is also a way to show ourselves, and others, that we have taste, we have "class". The objectives motivating us to consume A&C may be not just utilitarian or hedonic but symbolic as well, because the act of consuming lets us signal our identity—both to others and to ourselves.

In studying how A&C products are consumed, it is not enough to identify the key variables deriving from our proposed definition. We have to look further and find explanations. For example, why does Takumi hesitate before saying yes to his friend Frank? We can deduce from his diary that he does so because he does not like uncertainty. Therefore, we could form a hypothesis that Takumi's cognitive activity is influenced by a particular trait of his character.

Researchers in the field of cultural consumption, and in the social sciences, normally strive to explain any observed consumer activities in a manner that lets them develop knowledge and conclusions which can be generalized. For example, based on Takumi's story, we might argue that the more a consumer tends to avoid uncertainty, the more a situation perceived as uncertain will cause them to reflect longer before making a decision. To validate this hypothesis, we will examine whether this behaviour is repeated by other consumers, and perhaps with other products as well. Let us continue with this example: other researchers might argue it depends on the degree to which environmental factors can reassure the consumer. Doesn't Takumi say he accepted in the end because it was his friend Frank who asked him? Frank is thus a factor in Takumi's social environment which helps to diminish the effect of perceived uncertainty.

This, among other approaches, is how knowledge is developed in a given field of research. A researcher will observe a phenomenon that intrigues them, propose an explanation, and then put that explanation to the test in a formal study. The results will interest other researchers, who then formulate more refined explanations of what is being observed. And so, the cycle continues.

A CONCEPTUAL MODEL

Our proposed definition establishes that cultural consumption brings a number of variables, processes, and influences into play. To help us see through this complexity, it is useful to build a simplified representation or *model*. A model presents the basic elements of the generally complex phenomenon one is trying to understand. It serves to orient research and frame discussions about that phenomenon with the aid of a limited number of concepts.

Figure 1.1 A conceptual model for the consumption of arts and culture (A&C).

The model we will employ as our foundation for discussing cultural consumption appears in Figure 1.1. It contains three groups of variables: the psyche, the experience, and the social environment. Note that, apart from the introduction and conclusion, the different sections of this book follow the sequence of these groups: we examine the psyche in Chapter 2, the experience in Chapters 3 to 6, and the social environment in Chapter 7.

Let us briefly define these three groups of variables and then see how they help to give meaning to Takumi's description of his night at the opera.

The psyche

Every person is unique—we notice it every time we interact with other people. When we meet someone for the first time, we tend to form a natural impression of their character. For example, we will judge that a person is a little self-centred, or shy, or easy-going. The psyche is the sum of the relatively stable psychological characteristics which make a person unique and guide how they will behave in different situations. Takumi Suzuki defines himself as someone who is wary of things outside his knowledge; this seems to be a feature of his personality. He also says that formal dress is not to his liking. Our psyche can be studied from not only the perspective of how other people see us (personality) but also from the perspective of how we see ourselves (the concept of self or "self-concept"). These two aspects of the psyche—personality and self-concept—and their impact on A&C consumer behaviour are discussed in Chapter 2.

The experience

Takumi Suzuki's description of his night at the opera house contains multiple elements; it is not simply limited to buying a ticket and then watching the performance. For example, he hesitates to accept the invitation from his friend Frank, and he wonders how he should dress. He searches online for information about the opera, and he attends a pre-concert lecture by a musicologist so he can learn about the work and the composer. He experiences different emotions during the performance, is enamoured with the Sydney Opera House, and makes a plan to invite Frank to attend another opera with him. In a nutshell, the process of consuming A&C (focused, in our made-up story, on a very specific product: opera) generally includes a multitude of events that form what is called the *consumer experience*. In this book, we conceive of the consumer experience as a range of activities and processes grouped into four main categories: cognition (perception, reflection, inference), learning (associations, memory, socialization), affect (attitudes, emotions), and decision-making (search for information, evaluation of options, satisfaction). These topics are covered in Chapters 4 to 6.

The social environment

We cannot approach the study of consumer behaviour without mentioning the significant influence of the social environment. In a great many situations, the behaviour of consumers will, unquestionably, be influenced by the people who move within their social circle (such as friends, neighbours, colleagues), the people they admire or compare themselves to (family, community, membership groups, aspirational groups), or the people they want to dissociate from (take your pick—it depends on the person). This influence can exert itself in multiple forms. For example, a friend may share her impression of a play she attended (informational influence), or you may discover that a person you identify with is adopting certain behaviours (comparative influence). Thus, in our story, Takumi's friend Frank evidently plays an important role in his first encounter with the opera—as a source of information and certainly as a model of behaviour as well.

The social influence on consumer behaviour is often more subtle, however. For example, our belonging to a given society leads us to adopt certain ways of thinking and acting which are particular to that society's culture, and of which we may not even be aware. Takumi's negative attitude towards things he does not know can be interpreted not only as a feature of his personality but also as a facet of the society to which he belongs: in relative terms, members of Japanese society display a strong propensity to avoiding uncertainty. These and other related topics are discussed in Chapter 7.

PREMISES AND CHAPTER STRUCTURE

In writing this book, we have started from three basic premises. The first is that A&C consumers are similar to any other type of consumer. Some may argue their behaviour is more hedonic, or more symbolic as well, and one cannot compare the purchase of a toothbrush with, say, a visit to a museum. It is true that visiting a museum (to continue with this example) is symbolically charged and the experience is more hedonistic. It is equally true, however, that the processes underlying this consumer activity (perception, learning, decision-making, formation of attitudes, emotions, and so on) are the same as those which come into play when we purchase commodities. Therefore, the chapters of this book generally begin with a summary of the knowledge developed in the field of consumer behaviour, with the aim of providing conceptual foundations that may prove useful to our understanding of how A&C products are consumed.

The second premise is that the ultimate goal of consumer research in the field of A&C is to improve the performance of A&C organizations. This does not mean every study in this area should pursue this objective directly, but it is important to consider the practical implications of the knowledge we produce as researchers. Accordingly, each chapter of this book includes a section where we try to identify the practical implications of the research results we present.

The third and last premise is that much remains to be done in this field of research (see also Bourgeon-Renault, 2000). Scientific journals are very active in the field, research results are well disseminated, and more and more researchers are interested in this type of consumer behaviour, but many opportunities await for developing knowledge further. Therefore, each chapter also contains suggestions as to the direction future research can take and what issues it can explore and what theories and applications it can test.

REFERENCES

Bourgeon-Renault, D. (2000), "Evaluating Consumer Behaviour in the Field of Arts and Culture Marketing", *International Journal of Arts Management*, 3 (1), 4–18.

Colbert, F. (2014), "Introduction to the Special Issue on Marketing the Arts: The Arts Sector, A Marketing Definition", *Psychology & Marketing, Special Issue*, 31 (8), 563–565.

Colbert, F. (2017), "A Brief History of Arts Marketing Thought in North America", *Journal of Arts Management, Law and Society*, 47 (3), 167–177.

Colbert, F. and D. Dantas (2019), "Key Directions of Academic Research in Customer Relationships for Arts Marketing", *International Journal of Arts Management*, 21 (2), 4–14.

Colbert, F. and Y. St-James (2014), "Research in Arts Marketing: Evolution and Future Directions", *Psychology & Marketing*, 31 (8), 566–576.

Colbert, F. et al. (2018), *Marketing Culture and the Arts*, 5th edition, Montréal: Carmelle and Rémi Marcoux Chair in Arts Management.

Stuckey, A. (2020), "6 Effective Ways to Promote a Live Classical Music Concert" https://www.ticketsource.co.uk/blog/how-to-promote-your-classical-music-concert

THE PSYCHE

Part 2

Personality and self-concept
Chapter 2

Our discussion in this chapter focuses on two elements which partly define the consumer psyche: *personality* and *self-concept*. These two facets of the psyche have greatly influenced research into consumer psychology and behaviour. We can trace this influence to the belief, most likely *a priori*, that if one can identify the fundamental aspects of someone's character, one can predict their patterns of behaviour, especially those affecting their habits as a consumer—what activities they choose, what products or brands they prefer, and so on.

The multiple studies that have investigated the relationship between personality and consumer behaviour, or focused on self-concept, did not always yield the expected results, but they have nevertheless helped us identify the limits of the psyche as a predictive variable of consumer behaviour. Those studies have also opened avenues to innovative research approaches which marketers can apply to their work so as to understand the behaviour and satisfy the needs of their customers much more effectively.

PERSONALITY

Personality is a concept we commonly use to define people's character. For example, we often say that someone has "a nice personality" or we "don't like the personality" of someone else. When we refer to an individual's personality, we are activating a general impression in our mind that relies on a synthetic, global, and unique view of the person's psychological characteristics. If we are asked to explain further, we might say a person bothers us because she is self-centred, or we like her because she

DOI: 10.4324/9780429263118-4

cares about others, or we appreciate her dynamic style and bold attitude. Defining someone's personality, then, involves a recognition of their relatively stable character traits (e.g., dynamism, egocentricity, empathy, audacity), which presumably we have inferred from multiple observations. For example, a person who likes to show off their supposed expertise in art—"it's a Caravaggio, you know? What a pity . . . I could teach you so much about this extraordinary Italian painter if I only had the time to spare"—will most likely be perceived as narcissistic. Personality, then, can be defined as the set of relatively stable and permanent psychological characteristics which lead a person to display a consistent pattern of behaviour (d'Astous et al., 2018, p. 53).

Approaches in psychology

Research on personality has a long history in psychology. Many empirical studies completed in the 1950s sought to identify and measure the universal traits for defining the personality of any given individual. This research led to the creation of many original psychometric tests. The most well-known and widely used of these tests is certainly the Myers-Briggs Type Indicator (MBTI), the premise of which is to position any person among a set of 16 possible types. The validity of the Myers-Briggs and other such tests was strongly criticized. More recent and more rigorous studies have given rise to a theory of personality which, although not unanimously accepted, has met with approval from a very large number of researchers: the Five-Factor Model (FFM), also known as the Big Five Personality Test (see McRae and Costa, 2003). According to this theory, there are five fundamental dimensions of personality (as a mnemonic aid, their initials can form the words OCEAN or CANOE):

Conscientiousness: The tendency to adopt an organized and self-disciplined approach in dealing with our environment or, on the contrary, to act in a carefree or unreliable manner.
Agreeableness: The tendency to be altruistic and harmonious in our relations with others or, on the contrary, to be combative or detached.
Neuroticism: The tendency to approach things in a nervous way or, on the contrary, with confidence or emotional stability.

Openness to experience: The tendency to be cautious and look for what is familiar or, on the contrary, to be curious and look for what is new.

Extraversion: The tendency to be sociable (oriented towards the outside world) and energetic or, on the contrary, to be solitary (oriented towards the inside world) and reserved.

To measure where someone falls in each dimension and thus determine their personality type, researchers present the subject with a series of statements and invite them to indicate their level of agreement. For example, an agreeable person would tend to agree with the following statement: "I treat everyone with kindness and sympathy". In general, the five-factor theory has shown its usefulness in many areas of psychology (Cervone and Pervin, 2016).

Approaches in marketing

Research on personality in the field of psychology had a great influence on marketing researchers, mainly in the 1950s and 1960s. We can adduce several reasons for this influence. First, it seemed logical in that era to study consumer behaviour with the concepts then dominating the interest of psychology researchers, and personality was certainly one of those concepts. Second, the easy availability of personality tests, and the relatively simple method of administering them to consumers (who in many cases were students), made it possible for researchers to obtain data quickly and without much impediment. Also, the sets of data they collected were enormous and had to be analysed using multivariate statistical tools, such as multiple regression analysis and factor analysis, which were quite new for the time. These tools gave personality studies a certain aura of scientific authority—a significant attribute for the young discipline of marketing, which was concerned with making its mark in the humanities and social sciences. Last, we can be sure many researchers held the conviction that personality traits were a significant determining factor in the choice of products and brands.

A critical review of this literature, published in the early 1970s (Kassarjian, 1971), managed to upset this consensus by showing that not only did research in this field lack rigour but the capacity for personality to predict consumer behaviour was actually quite negligible. In the wake of this critical review, with the exception of a few studies that adopted the FFM (e.g., Mulyanegara et al., 2007), research on the relationship between personality and consumption practically sank beneath the waves.

The personality of consumption objects

In the late 1990s, marketing research into personality experienced a revival when experts began to focus on the "personality" of consumption objects like brands, stores, and websites. The concept behind this research stream is *anthropomorphism*, our natural tendency to attribute human personality traits to nonhuman objects such as animals or deities, or even to inanimate objects such as cars or musical instruments. One reason for this tendency is that we are naturally inclined to form an impression of others upon coming into contact with them. Thus, how we see any object is automatically filtered through an impression we have constructed. Another reason is that many of the objects around us possess attributes which remind us of human traits. In observing a cat, for example, we may say that he is mischievous or adventurous; in similar fashion, marketers and advertisers will often portray brands as people—think of the many characters like Mister Muffler or Aunt Jemima who exemplify how personification is used to make products, brands, and other consumer goods appear more human. Thus, to promote milk consumption, an advertisement might endow a cow with a human voice and expression; a brand which markets bold, distinctive products such as this will make a stronger impression on the minds of consumers.

Jennifer Aaker's work on brand personality (Aaker, 1997) has certainly had the most influence in this area of research. Her studies led her to conclude that the personality of brands, when viewed in general, includes five dimensions: Sincerity, Excitement, Competence, Sophistication, and Ruggedness. Researchers have also proposed personality scales for other consumption objects such as stores (d'Astous and Lévesque, 2003) and countries (d'Astous and Boujbel, 2007).

SELF-CONCEPT

We have seen that the purpose of personality research is to identify the stable character of a person (or another object) on the basis of a set of psychological characteristics that we call traits. This approach takes up an external, imposed perspective to view traits which are presumed to be universal. At the same time, we are privileged observers of our own selves in different situations. So our propensity to form impressions of the objects around us also applies to us. Thus, each person forms an image of themselves which researchers call a *self-concept*. It represents how we see ourselves—a perception of who we are (self-image) or who we wish to be (our ideal self) (Sirgy, 1982). We form this perception by not only observing how we ourselves behave (*I usually meet my deadlines, so I am a reliable person*) and how others behave in relation to us (*people usually greet me with a smile, so I must be a pleasant person*) but also from the information we receive about ourselves (*my friends say I am a little naive*).

Our self-concept plays a central role in defining our identity from a personal or social point of view. We are naturally inclined to consolidate this identity, to protect it, so we can live in harmony with ourselves. Consumption habits play a significant role in this respect, because products, brands, and other consumption objects act as signals conveying information about our identity to ourselves and to other people. Most marketing researchers believe that consumers' possessions (clothing, collections, photos, etc.) and the activities they engage in (concerts, museum visits, etc.) are an integral part of their self-concept (the "extended self") insofar as these elements reflect their identity—sometimes to an intense degree. Therefore, our consumption preferences are partly guided by our self-concept, whether real or idealized—the image we wish to convey to others and the one we convey to ourselves.

This latter statement refers to a very popular theory in marketing known as *self-image congruence* (Graeff, 1996). According to this theory, consumers are naturally inclined to prefer consumption objects (brands, products, shops, advertisements, etc.) which align with their self-concept. Researchers have verified this prediction in a large number of studies conducted in different situations (Onkvisit and Shaw, 1987). For example, d'Astous and Lévesque (2003) have shown that the more a store's personality matches that of consumers, the more their level of appreciation for that store increases.

PERSONALITY AND SELF-CONCEPT IN THE FIELD OF ARTS AND CULTURE

Researchers in cultural marketing have also taken a strong interest in personality and self-concept.

Personality, reading preferences, and musical tastes

A fairly abundant literature exists on the relationship connecting our personality with our reading preferences and musical tastes. A few scientific journals, such as *Psychology of Music*, even specialize in research studies investigating this type of relationship. As we saw in the previous section, marketing studies on personality date back to the 1950s and 1960s, and this is also true for research on the role of personality in reading and music.

Music

Let us examine some of the interesting results obtained in leading research studies on personality and musical taste. According to Schafer and Sedlmeier (2010), the type of music we listen to has a link to our identity and represents one of the elements reflecting our personality. Building on this conclusion, Bonetti and Costa (2016) showed that people who love music in the minor modes are more open to others, show greater empathy, and possess a fluid intelligence, with these traits leading them to prefer more complex musical genres such as classical. In a contemporaneous study, Greenberg et al. (2016) found that people who are more open to experience also prefer new, more complex, intense, and rebellious music.

Rentfrow et al. (2011) explored the relationships between the personality traits of sample groups and their entertainment preferences with respect to four categories of media: music, cinema, books, and television. In their study, two categories of taste emerged very clearly: on the one hand, people who consume mostly classical, jazz, or opera, as well as books relating to history, art, or science (commonly referred to as sophisticated or highbrow art products); on the other, people who enjoy action, suspense, or horror films, sitcoms, reality TV, and pop music (popular art products).

By associating preferences with personality more precisely, we can further analyse and refine the categories of this dichotomy between sophisticated and popular art. Let us take three examples of the five personality categories which according to Rentfrow et al. (2011) can be associated with entertainment preferences:

"Aesthetic entertainment": This category includes people who love entertainment which can be described as abstract, dense, and demanding. They appreciate what is creative, calm, and introspective and are in touch with their emotions.
"Cerebral entertainment": This category refers to people who prefer the brainier types of entertainment. They presumably have strong intelligence, and are extroverted, enterprising, innovative, intellectual, self-confident, and detail-oriented.
"Dark entertainment": People in this category are interested in dramatic, obscure, even gloomy entertainment objects. They tend to be defiant, reckless, and immodest.

In conclusion, Rentfrow et al. (2011) argue that consumers prefer such forms of entertainment that reflect aspects of their personality and are likely to reinforce their identity.

Reading

Schutte and Malouff (2004) investigated reading habits as a function of personality by applying the FFM we discussed briefly above (McRae and Costa, 2003), particularly with regard to the traits of openness, conscientiousness, and extraversion. A high degree of openness was shown to be associated with a preference for novels that refer to scholarly culture and the sciences, whereas a low degree of openness was associated with reading people-focused books, that is books which deal with themes more closely tied to immediate practical interests. Furthermore, a high level of conscientiousness was shown to be related to a preference for scientific literature as well as writings that concern events in society and around the world, such as political news. Last, the results of the study confirmed that the more extraverted a person is, the greater their interest in news and current affairs.

Personality, products, and brands

While human beings naturally attribute a personality to a product or brand, they do so for events, performance halls, and cities as well. In a study of 191 adult consumers, d'Astous et al. (2006) showed that festivals can be positioned according to five dimensions of personality: dynamism, sophistication, reputation, openness to the world, and innovation. The results of this study also showed that attendees who perceive a festival's personality to be similar to their own tend to evaluate the festival more favourably. A subsequent study by Ouellet et al. (2008) showed that we normally perceive performing arts centres in terms of either their prestige or their trendiness. Last, when viewed as tourist destinations, cities are seen as exciting, sincere, or friendly (Hosany et al., 2006).

Self-concept

According to self-image congruence theory, cultural consumers look for products which cohere with their self-concept. In the case of performance halls (prestigious or trendy), consumers tend to patronize venues which are consistent with their own perceived level of prestige or trendiness. They tend to negatively rate the venues they perceive as having more prestige than they do, but respond positively to those they see as being trendier than themselves (Ouellet et al., 2008). In addition, teenagers use the music they listen to as a way of asserting their identity—what they are or want to be, both for themselves and for others (Bonneville et al., 2013). With age, people become more resistant to peer pressure, and their self-concept moulds itself more closely to their new social roles. Life stages such as being a parent or making a career partly determine how our new personality traits take shape. This process could explain why, later in life, music acts less as an identifier for signalling our personality, and more as a tool for relaxing or regulating our emotions.

For some people, one way to signal their identity to others is to consume cultural products they perceive as *authentic*.

Authenticity is a complex, multidimensional concept that depends on the position of the person in relation to their reference group, to the objects, and to themselves. Regarding recorded music, for example, one is sometimes amazed by the rebirth of interest in the good old vinyl record. A significant aspect of this phenomenon is the search for authenticity, which can help individuals recognize themselves and at the same time project a self-image that positions them in relation to others. Two researchers, Goulding and Derbaix (2019), have studied the case of a vinyl record store in England. The store has been in existence since the 1950s and has an impressive collection of over 3,000 records. Its owners are always on the lookout for old and new records. They have a loyal customer base that combines appreciation of authenticity with personal vision. When these customers visit the store, they can converse with the staff and with other customers in a way that differentiates them from the rest of society. They think of themselves as experts who appreciate what is authentic, unlike people who regard an old vinyl record as merely an outdated object to throw in the trash.

In a later chapter, we will discuss the concepts of cultural capital and cultural omnivorousness. Suffice it to say for now that some consumers are animated by a desire to project the image of a person who can discern what is authentic from what is not—for example, who has the ability to appreciate authentic works of outsider art (Hahl et al., 2017). With more and more people (including those in the middle class) frequenting high-status cultural institutions, the act of appreciating sophisticated art becomes a less determining factor in the ability to distinguish oneself as elite. The distinction between social classes can therefore be made by the ability to disentangle what is authentic in popular art from what is not.

In conclusion, let us note the interesting results of a recent study (Michael, 2017) which examined a cohort of young European business professionals in managerial positions and their use of sophisticated art in defining their self-concept in relation to others. The author of this study reported that while these professionals say they are open to visiting museums and attending concerts, they do not see these activities as a form of distinction, but as a moral signal instead. They express a belief that they are morally "superior" because they are interested in what is acceptable to the elites, and not interested in the cultural objects which other social classes enjoy, such as "aggressive, weird or lazy music".

IMPLICATIONS FOR THE MARKETING OF ARTS AND CULTURE

What implications for managing a cultural organization can we draw from the concepts presented in this chapter? How can understanding personality and self-concept help a cultural organization meet the preferences of its target markets? First, it is important for any organization to know as much as possible about the motivations of the people in its target markets, including the factors that shape their preferences. This knowledge helps the organization adapt its message to each consumer market in terms of the preferences and reasons inspiring consumers to choose one cultural product over another. Thus, the organization can serve and convince consumers better because they understand them better. It is a waste of time, energy, and money to use arguments that run contrary to the preferences of potential customers or conflict with their self-concept. Capitalizing on the perceived benefits tying the fan to the cultural organization makes any promotional campaign more relevant. A target market typically consists of different segments. Each of these segments contains its own specific and distinct motivations for responding to the same product offering, for example, when they purchase tickets to a single event. If for one person the main reason to attend the opera is a desire for introspection, for another it may be above all a wish to signal their belonging to a particular social group. These two motivations may correspond to two market segments requiring different sales arguments.

If a market segment mostly contains people who need to distinguish themselves from others by their ability to judge what is authentic from what is not, then managers will have an interest in determining how to satisfy that need. It may represent an important market segment for the organization.

IMPLICATIONS FOR RESEARCH

In arts and culture, research on personality and self-concept has not progressed very far. This arises partly from a lack of interest among marketers in both of these elements of the consumer psyche but also *a fortiori* from a lack of knowledge about these concepts. In this chapter, we offered a synthesis aimed at showing their usefulness and motivating researchers to study these concepts in greater depth. In the following paragraphs, we suggest relevant avenues of research for consideration by any stakeholder in the field.

First, it appears to us that the FFM of personality has not generated as much interest as it deserves among researchers in the arts and culture field. In particular, it would be interesting to contrast the personality of cultural consumers according to a range of arts and culture products and using the appropriate measuring instruments (OCEAN). The product categories selected by d'Astous et al. (2008), in their multi-country study on the influence of country of origin, could serve as a basis for establishing such comparisons (sophisticated art and popular art). These categories were theatre, opera, classical music, art museums, action and adventure films, novels, comic books, classical ballet, and jazz music. Naturally, this list of artistic and cultural products can be expanded.

Second, although the proposition which holds that consumers naturally attribute personality traits to a variety of consumer goods has found some resonance in cultural marketing research (on festivals: d'Astous et al., 2006; on art venues: Ouellet et al., 2008), we nevertheless believe this proposition should be tested with other products. One benefit would be to fuel the thinking of marketing planners in cultural organizations as to how current and potential customers perceive the company or its brand, as well as those of its competitors; another benefit would be to determine the extent to which personality traits can be generalized to all cultural products or to subsets.

Last, it is very surprising that researchers in the field of arts and culture have so far shown very little interest in self-image congruence theory. This lack of interest contrasts sharply with the multiple applications of this theory in marketing (e.g., see Onkvisit and Shaw, 1987). In addition to the value of testing this theory with diverse categories of cultural products, we believe it is important that instruments of quality for measuring self-concept and consumer object dimensions be developed for use by marketers in cultural organizations.

REFERENCES

Aaker, J. L. (1997), "Dimensions of Brand Personality", *Journal of Marketing Research*, 34 (3), 347–356.

Bonetti, L. and M. Costa (2016), "Intelligence and Musical Mode Preference", *Empirical Studies of the Arts*, 34 (2), 160–176.

Bonneville, A., P. J. Rentfrow, M. K. Xu, and J. Potter (2013), "Music through the Ages: Trends in Musical Engagement and Preferences from Adolescence through Middle Adulthood", *Journal of Personality and Social Psychology*, 105 (4), 703–717.

Cervone, D. and L. A. Pervin (2016), *Personality: Theory and Research*, 13th edition, New York, NY: John Wiley & Sons.

d'Astous, A. and L. Boujbel (2007), "Positioning Countries on Personality Dimensions: Scale Development and Implications for Country Marketing," *Journal of Business Research*, 60 (3), 231–239.

d'Astous, A., F. Colbert, and E. d'Astous (2006), "The Personality of Cultural Festivals: Scale Development and Applications", *International Journal of Arts Management*, 8 (2), 14–23.

d'Astous, A., N. Daghfous, P. Balloffet, and C. Boulaire (2018), *Comportement du consommateur*, 5th edition, Montréal: Chenelière Éducation.

d'Astous, A., Z. Giraud Voss, F. Colbert, A. Carù, M. Caldwell, and F. Courvoisier (2008), "Product-Country Images in the Arts: A Multi-Country Study", *International Marketing Review*, 25 (4), 379–403.

d'Astous, A. and M. Lévesque (2003), "A Scale for Measuring Store Personality", *Psychology & Marketing*, 20 (5), 455–469.

Goulding, C. and M. Derbaix (2019), "Consuming Material Authenticity in the Age of Digital Reproduction", *European Journal of Marketing*, 53 (3), 545–564.

Graeff, T. R. (1996), "Image Congruence Effects on Product Evaluations", *Psychology & Marketing*, 13 (5), 481–499.

Greenberg, D. M., M. Kosinski, D. J. Stillwell, B. L. Monteiro, D. J. Levitin, and P. J. Rentfrow (2016), "The Song Is You: Preferences for Musical Attribute Dimensions Reflect Personality", *Social Psychological and Personality Science*, 7 (6), 597–605.

Hahl, O., E. W. Zuckerman, and M. Kim (2017), "Why Elites Love Authentic Lowbrow Culture: Overcoming High-Status Denigration with Outsider Art", *American Sociological Review*, 82 (4), 828–856.

Hosany, S., Y. Ekinci, and M. Uysal (2006), "Destination Image and Destination Personality: An Application of Brand theories to Tourism Places", *Journal of Business Research*, 59 (5), 638–642.

Kassarjian, H. H. (1971), "Personality and Consumer Behavior: A Review", *Journal of Marketing Research*, 8 (4), 409–418.

McRae, R. R. and P. T. Costa (2003), *Personality in Adulthood: A Five-Factor Theory Perspective*, 2nd edition, New York, NY: Guilford Press.

Michael, J. (2017), "Highbrow Culture for High-Potentials? Cultural Orientations of a Business Elite in the Making", *Poetics*, 61, 39–52.

Mulyanegara, R. C., Y. Tsarenko, and A. Anderson (2007), "The Big Five and Brand Personality: Investigating the Impact of Consumer Personality on Preferences towards Particular Brand Personality", *Journal of Brand Management*, 16 (4), 234–247.

Onkvisit, S. and J. Shaw (1987), "Self-Concept and Image Congruence: Some Research and Managerial Issues", *Journal of Consumer Marketing*, 4 (1), 13–23.

Ouellet, J. F., M-A. Savard, and F. Colbert (2008), "The Personality of Performing Arts Venues: Developing a Measurement Scale", *International Journal of Arts Management*, 10 (3), 49–59.

Rentfrow, P. J., L. R. Goldberg, and R. Zilca (2011), "Listening, Watching, and Reading: The Structure and Correlates of Entertainment Preferences", *Journal of Personality*, 79 (2), 223–257.

Schafer, T. and P. Sedlmeier (2010), "What Makes Us Like Music? Determinants of Music Preference", *Psychology of Aesthetics, Creativity, and the Arts*, 4 (4), 223–234.

Schutte, N. S. and J. M. Malouff (2004), "University Student Reading Preferences in Relation to the Big Five Personality Dimensions", *Reading Psychology*, 25 (4), 273–295.

Sirgy, M. J. (1982), "Self-concept in Consumer Behavior: A Critical Review", *Journal of Consumer Research*, 9 (3), 287–300.

EXERIENCE
Part 3

Perception

Chapter 3

In marketing and social sciences, it is common to view perception as a process one can define with a set of steps and a clear linear sequence (e.g., Solomon, 2017). This view holds that a variety of stimuli (images, sounds, odours, etc.) reach the senses of the consumer (sight, hearing, taste, smell, and touch) before being selected, organized, and then interpreted by the brain. This sequence constitutes what is called the *perceptual experience*.

Although, as we shall see further on, this view of perception is not consistent with many results from psychology research—notably, that perception is usually immediate and deep—it is useful for how it distinguishes three fundamental themes one must integrate into any discussion of perceptual experience: selective perception, perceptual organization, and interpretation. We will address each of these themes in turn.

SELECTIVE PERCEPTION

Consumers are exposed to a considerable number of stimuli of all kinds. It is logically impossible for them to take everything into account, so they must be selective. The process of selecting information in the environment is either voluntary (e.g., a given person may choose to mute the ad appearing on her smartphone before the broadcast of a news report) or involuntary (e.g., when we hear a fire alarm being triggered). Beyond these two obvious conditions of selective perception, there also exists a process of automatic selection, that is, selection based on a person's objectives, motivations, or psychic state. For example, a consumer who likes a particular brand will tend to perceive

DOI: 10.4324/9780429263118-6

(and no doubt also remember) more positive information in that brand's advertising than will a different person who is resistant to it. From this perspective, it becomes clear that perception is a fundamentally individual process.

In this context, it is useful to distinguish between two types of factors that influence selective perception: structural and motivational (Krech and Crutchfield, 1972). Structural factors, the first type, refer to the physical nature of stimuli present in the environment in such great variety—for example, their size, intensity, colour, position in the field of view, order of presentation, degree of difference from surrounding stimuli (contrast), level of ambiguity, negativity, and concrete character. Their effects on selective perception are well documented in the literature on consumer behaviour (e.g., d'Astous et al., 2018). These effects are often predictable (e.g., the greater the stimulus, the more likely it is to be perceived), but sometimes unexpected (e.g., negative information has more impact than positive information).

Motivational factors, the second type, refer not to the physical environment but to the characteristics of the consumer—more precisely, to their needs, preferences, and emotional state. For example, consumers who are in a good mood have a more positive perception of service quality (Chebat et al., 1995). The effects of motivational factors on consumer perceptions are also well documented in the literature (d'Astous et al., 2018).

PERCEPTUAL ORGANIZATION

The stimuli which surround consumers are not only numerous but are unorganized *a priori* as well. Anyone who has had the experience of arriving in a foreign country where the writing system and native language are unknown to them will certainly know the disorienting feeling of not being able to even distinguish or read, let alone understand, the written characters on signs and billboards. They are incomprehensible for that person, of course, but not for the local people. Individual written characters (i.e., graphemes) are grouped in our minds to form words, phrases, and ideas through the process of perceptual organization. It is also through the process of perceptual organization that successive sounds become melodies, or strokes of paint form an image conveying a personal meaning. Therefore, to understand perception, it is necessary to understand how the minds of consumers organize stimuli from their environment in a coherent way. One key to this understanding is a fundamental mental process called *categorization*.

Consumers naturally group objects in their environment into more or less general mental categories. In this way, they reduce the inherent complexity of their environment and enable themselves to interact with it more effectively. Rather than forming distinct and unique terms to describe the objects in our environment (e.g., a painting which represents a landscape through purposely indistinct forms, bright colours, tricks of light, etc.), we place the objects in mental categories—or *concepts*—on the basis of their similarity (e.g., the concept of impressionist painting). Objects that belong to a mental category tend to resemble each other (a process of assimilation), whereas those associated with different mental categories tend to distinguish themselves (a process of contrast). Although objects in the environment can be categorized at different levels of specificity (e.g., a Turner-style impressionist painting, an impressionist painting, a painting), several studies in psychology have shown that people categorize objects in their environment at an intermediate level of specificity called the *basic level* (Rosch, 1978). This level is neither too abstract (a painting) nor too concrete (a Turner-style impressionist painting), so as to make the categorization process more efficient.

Beyond the benefit of simplifying environmental stimuli through assimilation and contrast, categorization facilitates the inference process. When consumers place objects in a given mental category, they naturally assign the attributes of that category to the categorized objects. This process is called *stereotyping*. For example, a concert offered as part of the Montreal International Jazz Festival (the mental category) is likely to automatically generate inferences such as grandiose, urban, touristic, popular, festive, and outdoor. The categorization of an object allows the association of category-specific meanings with that object, which both enriches and guides the perceptual experience. One of the most important mental categories in the context of consumption is the brand name. A brand name not only serves to distinguish a product (in a broad sense) from competing products but also allows marketers to activate multiple inferences in the minds of consumers with regards to the quality, benefits, and satisfaction they can expect to obtain by purchasing and using that product.

INTERPRETATION

It seems incongruous to deal with the interpretation of stimuli after presenting the concepts of selective perception and perceptual organization. Essentially, the interpretation of stimuli—in other words, the process which gives them meaning—appears to be inseparable from the psychological mechanisms underlying their selection and organization in our mind. This is an important limitation upon conceiving perception on the basis of a step-by-step model (selection → organization → interpretation). Fortunately, we can free ourselves from this inadequate representation of perception by employing a central concept in consumer psychology and behaviour: the schema.

To introduce this concept, let us consider the following text:

> The procedure is actually quite simple. First you arrange things into different groups. Of course, one pile may be sufficient depending on how much there is to do. If you have to go somewhere else due to lack of facilities that is the next step, otherwise you are pretty well set. It is important not to overdo things. That is, it is better to do too few things at once than too many. In the short run this may not seem important but complications can easily arise. A mistake can be expensive as well. At first the whole procedure will seem complicated. Soon, however, it will become just another facet of life. After the procedure is completed one arranges the materials into different groups again. Then they can be put into their appropriate places. Eventually they will be used once more and the whole cycle will then have to be repeated. However, that is part of life.

This text probably appears somewhat obscure to you, and you may not understand what it is about. Two researchers in cognitive psychology read this text (slightly adapted here) to study participants and then measured their level of understanding (Bransford and Johnson, 1972). For half of the participants in this well-known study, the text was presented with no introduction or explanation, while for the other half it was preceded by the following sentence: "The paragraph you will hear will be about washing clothes". As one can imagine, the group that had the benefit of this title showed a significantly higher level of understanding than the other group. In providing a title, researchers knew they would be activating a familiar knowledge structure—the "laundry schema"—and this would help participants interpret the text better.

A schema is a pattern of thought—a mental structure—which includes knowledge, feelings, and images about an object (in a broad sense). There are several kinds of schema: those for people (e.g., conductor, ballerina), those for events (a night at the opera, a visit to a museum), those for places (a marquee, a theatre), and so on. These patterns—or *schemata*, in the plural—are constructed throughout our lives by the experiences we live through and the information we are exposed to. They act on the perceptual process in three ways: (1) by guiding the selection of information in the environment, (2) by facilitating inferences, and (3) by directing the retrieval of information from the memory.

The schema concept makes it possible to propose a model of perception which is more interesting than the step-by-step model we discussed earlier. This model was conceived by the American cognitive psychologist Ulric Neisser (1976), who argued that perception is essentially an active process of construction rooted in schema-driven expectations. Neisser's perceptual cycle model (PCM) is shown in Figure 3.1. In this model, the schema operates as a structure for our expectations: fundamentally, we perceive what we are seeking.

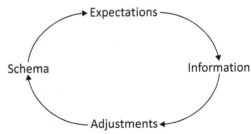

Figure 3.1 The perceptual cycle (from Neisser, 1976).

The schema guides the exploration stage, where new data are collected that will serve in turn for modifying the schema (to update or improve it), and this gives rise to a new schema and more exploration. The cycle repeats itself in this constant fashion, to create and renew the basis for perceptual experience.

The perceptual cycle offers a useful explanation for the phenomenon of how individuals appropriate a work of art (Carù and Cova, 2005). Consider, for illustration purposes, the case of someone listening to a new music piece—say, a work of contemporary classical music. The perceptual cycle proposes that before listening, the person activates one or more schemata that seem appropriate to him. A person who has already listened to such compositions may, for example, think of musical structures that are complex, non-melodic, or even atonal. If the listening is done live, during a concert, the view of the instruments assembled on the stage (brass, synthesizer, digital organ, etc.) can contribute to the activation of various schemata. As soon as the baton falls, these schemata, by means of the exploration process, will spur the listener to begin constructing a first interpretation of the work. This interpretation will evolve according to changes made to the schemata on the basis of musical information collected throughout the listening session. Carù and Cova (2005) have shown that the appropriation of an object of art, such as a work of classical music, can be shaped by the conductor's contextualization of the work. One can assume that any comments conveyed by the conductor may influence the nature of the schemata activated during listening, the selection of musical information by listeners, and the interpretation and overall appreciation they form in their minds.

PERCEPTION IN THE FIELD OF ARTS AND CULTURE

Several dimensions of perception, some addressing the notion of inference, have been explored in the field of arts and culture. In this section, we shall cover the following dimensions: perception of causality, risk, price and quality (respectively), and incorrect inferences.

Perception of causality

Consumers are not passive recipients in relation to the information and events that arise in their environment; they seek to give them meaning and identify their causes. To do so, they develop mental representations (schemata) which allow them, for example, to recognize they are being targeted by influencers (Friestad and Wright, 1994) or more generally to help them make decisions.

The impact of film criticism on consumer judgement provides a relevant example. Studies show that film-lovers do not necessarily rely on the views of film critics (d'Astous and Colbert, 2002; d'Astous and Touil, 2000). It may turn out that the assessment being made depends more on the context than the film itself. For example, if a certain critic has a habit of always praising a certain director, a consumer might perceive such praise as consistent with the prejudices of that critic. But if the critic issues a negative review while generally welcoming that director's work, the review may have a greater impact because of its distinctive character. So, it would not be a negative recommendation as such that influences the film-lover, but the fact that this critic has deviated from his normal habit, leading to the inference that his criticism must be taken seriously.

Another example is sponsorship in the world of arts and culture. Sponsorship involves financially supporting an artistic or cultural project (a festival, a series of concerts, a museum, etc.) in exchange for the possibility of exploiting this partnership for commercial purposes (Carrillat and d'Astous, 2015). When consumers perceive the sponsorship grounds as altruistic (i.e., as having the interests of the sponsored project at heart), their attitude towards the sponsoring company or brand will be more favourable than if they perceive the sponsor's objectives as primarily commercial (i.e., to promote its brand and products). Depending on the case, consumers will therefore attribute either philanthropic or commercial motives to the sponsor. In an experimental study on the impact of the sponsor type (private company, state-owned enterprise, or government department) and the nature of the sponsorship (philanthropic or commercial) in relation to consumer attitudes, it was found that people view philanthropic cultural sponsorships more favourably than those where the sponsor seems driven by a desire to promote its products (Colbert et al., 2005; d'Astous et al., 2005). The results of this study revealed that consumers view cultural sponsorships by private companies more positively than those by state-owned enterprises and value those by government departments last among these three types.

Perceived risk

In our modern societies, leisure time is not increasing—it is even decreasing, for certain categories of people (Colbert et al., 2018). It has become a precious commodity, just like the disposable income they have, so it is important to make the right choices. For example, purchasing a show ticket is a serious decision for many people, since it involves different risks and possible negative consequences. Performance risk: will the show meet their expectations? Economic risk: will the ticket be refunded if it becomes impossible for them to attend the show? Security risk: is the venue safe? Social risk: will the other spectators be courteous? Psychological risk: will the show contain disturbing scenes? Any consumption situation can be viewed through different dimensions of risk. What appears risky for one person will seem insignificant for another; risk is an individual psychological experience.

Because artistic and cultural products have a higher level of intangibility (Fraser et al., 2004), they are more likely to be perceived as risky. Studies show that as consumers learn more about an intangible product (as their level of knowledge increases), the perceived risk decreases because they can judge that product from their reservoir of product knowledge and brand familiarity (Nepomuceno et al., 2014). The less the consumer knows about the product, the more they have to rely on external sources of information to assess this risk, such as reading reviews or listening to what trusted people say. Thus, generally speaking, a classic play presented by a well-known theatre company in a prestigious venue, under a renowned director and with veteran performers, is less of a perceived risk than a creative show presented in an alternative theatre by an avant-garde company which no critic has reviewed and nobody knows. Depending on their personal tastes, however, a spectator might very well end up disliking the classic play, despite its low level of apparent risk, and be pleasantly surprised by the unknown play that posed a greater risk in advance. Similarly, a theatre fan who is familiar with new trends in theatrical performance will remain within their comfort zone in the second case. Risk perception applies to every cultural product, be it a novel, a new CD, a pop concert, a new exhibition, and so on.

Price perception

In the arts, the price encompasses notions of money, time, and perceived risk all at once. A price will be judged fair if it corresponds to an expected quality. The value of a product or an experience corresponds to an assessment of what is being received versus what it costs, either monetarily or psychologically (Zeithaml, 1988). Festivalgoers will be loyal to an event if they feel they will live an experience that matches or exceeds what they must expend in time or money (Tanford and Jung, 2017). This value is due as much to the hedonic characteristics of the festival as to the quality of the tourist infrastructure and the attraction of the locale where it takes place (Wu, 2016). Thus, the greater the perceived value, the more the festivalgoer will perceive the ticket price to be reasonable. One can go even further and say that the more positive the perception of an event (e.g., a festival), the more the consumer will want to share their satisfaction with those they know (word-of-mouth) and the more they will feel they have received value for money (positive price perception); these perceptions will condition them to accept a higher entry price the next time. They may even feel they have enjoyed a good bargain (Bergel and Brock, 2019).

Wiggins and Cui (2013) showed it to be more profitable, in certain circumstances, to let spectators decide by themselves the price to pay for attending a concert. In their study, four price conditions were tested: (1) no suggested price, with the spectator giving what he wants; (2) the suggestion of a maximum price; (3) the suggestion of a minimum price; and (4) the suggestion of an average price. The researchers found that greater box office receipts are produced if the consumers are allowed to decide what they want to pay, based on the value they give to the show (there was no suggested price). In this way the consumers can express their satisfaction according to an internal rule of their own. We should note this study was conducted in a closed environment. Generally, other theatres display a range of price categories and so the consumer has a base of reference for judging the amount to pay. For example, one might question what the consequences would be if all theatres suggested ticket buyers simply pay what they want. Would ticket buyers lose their bearings and end up driving box office receipts down? Or would those receipts perhaps be higher? Unless one carries out a field experiment, it will be very hard to ascertain.

However, at least one study tried to determine the average price a sample of spectators recalled having paid for their tickets in the previous year (Ravanas and Colletti, 2010). Surprisingly, the estimated price was on average 10% higher than the actual ticket price. One might therefore conclude that, in the case of this particular theatre, the audience were very satisfied and might agree to pay a higher price for their tickets.

In museum management, allowing free admission is a regularly discussed topic. The idea here is to attract more visitors, especially those categorized as city residents who do not attend museums. The study by Le Gall-Ely et al. (2008) showed that while some people may perceive free admission as eliminating a barrier to entry and encouraging them to attend, other people view payment of an admission fee as a contribution in support of the arts.

Perception of quality

Purchasing decisions are based on perceptions, and these perceptions somehow become reality. Someone who has no experience of a product will tend to use extrinsic attributes (e.g., theatre reputation), whereas someone who is familiar with the product will rely on its intrinsic qualities (e.g., quality of the actors). In the arts, new products generally hold sway, in the sense that the products being delivered are never exactly the same as earlier ones. Artists aim to surpass themselves, to explore new avenues. That is why, even when staging a classic play, theatre directors will seek to put their own stamp on the production—they will not want to repeat what others have done. Fans may know the play as written, but they will not be familiar with this new production. So they will tend to make their purchasing decision on the basis of extrinsic attributes.

For example, they may tell themselves that if the theatre decides to add extra performances, it must be because the shows were sold out, meaning the play must be very good (of high quality) and previous audiences must be very satisfied. In fact, a study of eight Montreal theatres showed that many potential spectators are willing to pay more for a show which is posting additional performances than for the same show in the regular season (Colbert et al., 1998). The reason they provide: they do not have much time to devote to leisure activities, and so they want to be sure they are making the right choice (quality). The fact that the show can advertise extra performances thus diminishes the perceived risk.

Another study (Voss and Cova, 2006), this one conducted with the audiences of two theatres in the United States, provides a further example of the effect of perceptions on satisfaction. The results of this study show that women are generally more satisfied if they perceive the theatre displays progressive social values. They take this extrinsic attribute into account when they evaluate different theatres. As for men, they differ in generally being more satisfied if they feel they are receiving a high level of customer service. Women and men therefore classify the quality of theatres according to different perceived attributes.

Incorrect inferences

Inferences are useful to consumers because they serve as a guide in the product evaluation process. These consumer inferences can be positive, neutral, or negative. They do not necessarily reflect reality, however. For example, consider the perception that young people have of museums. Researchers have shown that some young people perceive museums as places for people who love the arts, for cultivated people who have class and are sophisticated, or for "arty-farty" people who want to show off their appreciation of the arts (Mason and McCarthy, 2006). These youths also see them as places for older, wealthier, more educated people. Of course, we are dealing here with a selective perception which, without being very distant from reality, is nevertheless wrong. This false perception is one probable factor keeping young people away from museums, because these institutions do not reflect their identity, tastes, lifestyles, and concerns or the image they want to project to others. This is an incorrect inference which museum directors would certainly not agree with. In marketing and consumer behaviour, perception is, sometimes unfortunately, reality.

Another example of incorrect inference comes from the realm of cinema. Perception plays an important role in what people from different countries think of the films marketed by one of these countries. This perception can be both positive and negative. Bollywood films are an interesting case (Matuzitz and Payano, 2011). People in India tend to find that Bollywood films present a negative image of Muslim culture (negative inference). At the same time, they all agree these films represent a national treasure and must be preserved (positive inference). Americans, for their part, see these films as combining exotic locations, colourful costumes, and a temporary release from reality (escapism). It is therefore a positive inference if these attributes are pleasing, but negative if they are not, without necessarily reflecting the reality.

IMPLICATIONS FOR THE MARKETING OF ARTS AND CULTURE

Perception is a complex process that influences all aspects of consumer life (assessment, decision-making, communication, etc.). This is true in the cultural field as in any other area of the economy. The first lesson one can elicit concerns the preconceptions held by marketers vis-à-vis the potential spectators. Consumers do not necessarily follow a logical and Cartesian process when making a decision. They make inferences, they care about what others think, and they "manage" their emotions. Each person has their own way of working, depending on the knowledge and experience they have accumulated. The complexity of human beings should motivate us to avoid viewing the market in monolithic terms—and see it as a heterogeneous ensemble instead. Some market segments are defined by how the consumers within them make decisions. In the case of a hedonic product such as art, the customer seeks an enriching experience, both intellectually and in terms of pleasure or social interaction. Since perceived risk and perceived quality colour every decision, it is important that marketing managers be equipped to provide information capable of minimizing both types of perceived risk. The quality of a show or an exhibition will not be defined in the same way by different people. Some do not have the tools to assess the quality of a work in a meaningful way. They may think that because a certain prestigious conductor is leading the orchestra, the performance will be better, even if objectively it is not. Knowing the different elements that guide consumers' decisions is therefore of paramount importance—especially since, as we have already mentioned, the customer does not know in advance what the artistic product will be.

IMPLICATIONS FOR RESEARCH

Apart from the study by Carù and Cova (2005) on contemporary classical music, there is no research that has considered the perception of arts and culture products through the lens of Neisser's perceptual cycle model (1976). Yet this model offers a vision of perception that fits well with the nature of these products: often complex, unpredictable, and innovative. It seems especially worthwhile to study how one can facilitate the appropriation of artistic products by consumers who do not possess the necessary schemata for understanding and appreciating them. For example, how can experimental theatre novices be brought to decipher the meaning of an anticonformist play and possibly derive pleasure from seeing it? Studies have shown that when consumers are faced with products with a high degree of ambiguity, they tend to align their perceptions and assessments with the information transmitted by advertising (Hoch and Ha, 1986). On the other hand, if they are provided with effective "cognitive weapons" through a consumption vocabulary (i.e., the schemata), their understanding and appreciation of a seemingly complex product can be improved (d'Astous and Kamau, 2010; West et al., 1996). Anyone who has had the experience of observing an abstract painting in company with an experienced museum guide who skilfully describes the multiple elements that make the work meaningful will understand the inherent power of the schema to facilitate understanding. Although the strategy of passing on consumption vocabulary has long been known and used by the arts and culture community (e.g., personal or audio guides, presentation brochures, programme notes), this has not been the subject of systematic research.

As mentioned, the complexity of artistic and cultural products and their intangible aspects are factors that have a significant impact on perceived risk. It is strange that researchers in the field have not studied the determinants of perceived risk and the various strategies that can be deployed to reduce it. What means of reducing risk do arts and culture consumers favour? Do these methods vary according to the type of product? Does the type of risk (financial, psychological, social, etc.) also lead to variation? What is the relative effectiveness of these means, according to the segments of the target market? These are important questions for which we do not currently have answers.

REFERENCES

Bergel, M. and C. Brock (2019), "Visitors' Loyalty and Price Perceptions: The Role of Customer Engagement", *The Service Industries Journal*, 39 (7–8), 575–589.

Bransford, J. D. and M. K. Johnson (1972), "Contextual Prerequisites for Understanding", *Journal of Verbal Learning and Verbal Behavior*, 11, 717–726.

Carrillat, F. A. and A. d'Astous (2015), "Sponsorship", in N. Lee and A. Farrell (eds.), *Wiley Encyclopedia of Management*, 3rd edition, Vol. 9 (Marketing), pp. 1–7.

Carù, A. and B. Cova (2005), "The Impact of Service Elements on the Artistic Experience: The Case of Classical Music Concerts", *International Journal of Arts Management*, 7 (2), 39–54.

Chebat, J.-C., P. Filiatrault, C. Gélinas-Chebat, and A. Vanisky (1995), "Impact of Waiting Attribution and Consumer's Mood on Perceived Quality", *Journal of Business Research*, 34 (3), 191–196.

Colbert, F., A. d'Astous, and M.-A. Parmentier (2005), "Consumer Perception of Private versus Public Sponsorship of the Arts", *International Journal of Arts Management*, 8 (1), 48–60.

Colbert, F., L. Vallée, and C. Beauregard (1998), "The Importance of Ticket Prices for Theatre Patrons", *International Journal of Arts Management*, 1 (1), 8–15.

Colbert, F., et al. (2018), *Marketing Culture and the Arts*, 5th edition, Montreal: Carmelle and Rémi-Marcoux Chair in Arts Management.

Correia Loureiro, S. M., H. Roschk, and F. Lima (2019), "The Role of Background Music in Visitors' Experience of Art Exhibitions: Music, Memory and Art Appraisal", *International Journal of Arts Management*, 22 (1), 4–24.

d'Astous, A. and F. Colbert (2002), "Moviegoers' Consultation of Critical Reviews: Psychological Antecedents and Consequences", *International Journal of Arts Management*, 5 (1), 24–35.

d'Astous, A., F. Colbert, and M.-A. Parmentier (2005), "Consumer Perceptions of Sponsorship in the Arts: A Canadian Perspective", *International Journal of Cultural Policy*, 11 (2), 215–228.

d'Astous, A., N. Daghfous, P. Balloffet, and C. Boulaire (2018), *Comportement du consommateur*, 5ᵉ édition, Montréal: Chenelière Éducation.

d'Astous, A. and E. Kamau (2010), "Consumer Product Evaluation Based on Tactile Sensory Information", *Journal of Consumer Behavior*, 9, 206–213.

d'Astous, A. and N. Touil (2000), "Consumer Evaluations of Movies on the Basis of Critics' Judgment", *Psychology & Marketing*, 16 (8), 677–694.

Fraser, P., F. Kerrigan, and M. Özbilgin (2004), "Key Issues in Arts Marketing", in F. Kerrigan, P. Fraser and M. Özbilgin (eds.), *Arts Marketing*, London: Routledge, pp. 187–197.

Friestad, M. and P. Wright (1994), "The Persuasion Knowledge Model: How People Cope with Persuasion Attempts", *Journal of Consumer Research*, 21 (1), 1–31.

Hoch, S. J. and Y.-W. Ha (1986), "Consumer Learning: Advertising and the Ambiguity of Product Experience", *Journal of Consumer Research*, 13 (2), 221–233.

Krech, D. and R. S. Crutchfield (1972), "Perceiving the World", in J. B. Cohen (ed.), *Behavioral Science Foundations of Consumer Behavior*, Englewood Cliffs, NJ: Prentice Hall, pp. 147–160.

Le Gall-Ely, M., C. Urbain, D. Bourgeon-Renault, A. Gombault, and C. Petr (2008), "Free Admission to Museums and Monuments: An Exploration of Some Perceptions of the Audiences", *International Journal of Nonprofit and Voluntary Sector Marketing*, 13 (1), 57–72.

Mason, D. D. M. and C. McCarthy (2006), "'The Feeling of Exclusion': Young Peoples' Perceptions of Art Galleries", *Museum Management and Curatorship*, 21 (1), 20–31.

Matuzitz, J. and P. Payano (2011), "The Bollywood in Indian and American Perceptions: A Comparative Analysis", *India Quarterly*, 67 (1), 65–77.

Neisser, U. (1976), *Cognition and Reality*, San Francisco, CA: Freeman.

Nepomuceno, M. V., M. Laroche, and M.-O. Richard (2014), "How to Reduce Perceived Risk when Buying Online: The Interactions between Intangibility, Product Knowledge, Brand Familiarity, Privacy, and Security Concerns", *Journal of Retailing and Consumer Services*, 21 (4), 619–629.

Ravanas, P. and P. Colletti (2010), "A Ticket to Wonderland: Lookingglass Theatre Weathers the Recession with Clever Pricing", *International Journal of Arts Management*, 12 (3), 70–87.

Rosch, E. (1978), "Principles of Categorization", in E. Rosch and B. B. Lloyd (eds.), *Cognition and Categorization*, Hillsdale, IL: Erlbaum, pp. 27–48.

Solomon, M. R. (2017), *Consumer Behavior: Buying, Having, and Being*, 12th edition, Upper Saddle River, NJ: Pearson Education.

Tanford, S. and S. Yung (2017), "Festival Attributes and Perceptions: A Meta-Analysis of Relationships with Satisfaction and Loyalty", *Tourism Management*, 61, 209–220.

Voss, Z. and V. Cova (2006), "How Sex Differences in Perceptions Influence Customer Satisfaction: A Study of Theatre Audiences", *Marketing Theory*, 6, 201–221.

West, P. M., C. L. Brown, and S. J. Hoch (1996), "Consumption Vocabulary and Preference Formation", *Journal of Consumer Research*, 23 (2), 120–135.

Wiggins, J. and A. P. Cui (2013), "To Influence or Not to Influence: External Reference Price Strategies in Pay-What-You-Want Pricing", *Journal of Business Research*, 66 (2), 275–281.

Wiggins, J. and P. E. Grimm (2010), "Communal and Exchange Relationship Perceptions as Separate Constructs and Their Role in Motivations to Donate", *Journal of Consumer Psychology*, 20 (3), 282–294.

Wu, S.-I. (2016), "The Correlation between Factors in Festival Marketing Activities, Visitors' Value Perception and Post-Purchase Feelings", *Journal of Management and Sustainability*, 6 (4), 9–21.

Zeithaml, V. (1988), "Consumer Perceptions of Price, Quality, and Value: A Means-End Model and Synthesis of Evidence", *Journal of Marketing*, 52 (3), 2–22.

Learning

Chapter 4

In the previous chapter, we looked at a fundamental process of the consumer experience: perception. The logical continuation of that discussion is to examine what consumers derive from their perceptual experiences—what they learn. Our discussion is organized first around three different and complementary conceptions of the consumer learning process: the behavioural approach, the cognitive approach, and socialization. We will then examine results of research on this theme in the field of arts and culture, more specifically through the lens of socialization which the majority of studies have employed. The last two sections of the chapter discuss some implications for arts and culture managers and for researchers in the field.

CONSUMERS ARE LEARNERS BY NATURE

How behaviourists view learning

For most people, learning is about analysing information from the environment in order to produce knowledge. Children, for example, will learn to read a musical score by applying the rules their solfeggio teacher has put in front of them. So, for most of us, learning requires some mental effort. Any discussion of learning should therefore refer to mental activities.

Behaviourists think otherwise; they believe there is no need to refer to the mind when describing a large number of learning situations. In their view, it is sufficient simply to consider the effects of environmental factors on behaviour. At the heart of this stimulus–response approach are two behavioural theories of learning: classical conditioning and instrumental conditioning.

DOI: 10.4324/9780429263118-7

Classical conditioning

The central idea of classical conditioning is that consumers learn by making associations. For example, a classical music lover would learn Yannick Nézet-Séguin is an exceptional conductor, after enjoying the musical experience of attending a concert or listening to a recording by an orchestra under his direction. The more numerous and consistent such experiences are, the stronger the association becomes, and the more the conductor's name alone will evoke positive musical impressions.

This simple idea is of particular interest when the association process involves stimuli that are *a priori* neutral. To illustrate, let us imagine that Yamaha, the manufacturing conglomerate, has hired Yannick Nézet-Séguin as a spokesman for their brand of high-fidelity audio devices. By combining this conductor (the unconditioned stimulus) in a contiguous and repeated manner—for example, through advertising—with the Yamaha brand name (the conditioned stimulus), the positive musical experiences evoked by the conductor will eventually be transferred to the Yamaha brand. This classical conditioning process is illustrated in Figure 4.1.

For classical conditioning to work, conditioned and unconditioned stimuli must be presented together repeatedly. In the example above, which refers to the strategy of using a celebrity to influence a brand's image, the Yamaha brand name alone will evoke the impression of a rewarding musical experience if both mechanisms (contiguity and repetition) are implemented.

Classical conditioning finds its most common applications in the field of marketing communications when the objective is to

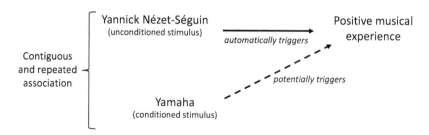

Figure 4.1 The classical conditioning process.

associate brands or given consumption situations with positive responses. For example, images of scenic landscapes will be used to promote a tourist site; images of children will be used to encourage charitable giving; and images of athletes will be used to create an impression of high performance.

A related phenomenon that is highly interesting: the responses which result from a classical conditioning process can be generalized to stimuli which are different from the conditioned stimuli but resemble them. This is called *stimulus generalization*. For example, any high-fidelity audio device which resembles one made by Yamaha is likely to cause reactions similar to those which consumers have learned through classical conditioning.

Instrumental conditioning

Classical conditioning takes a passive view of learning, one that sees consumers as being limited to making associations. But much of our learning is accomplished through a diverse range of experience. Instrumental conditioning (also known as *operant conditioning*) is a behavioural theory based on the idea that humans learn to engage in actions with positive consequences and to avoid actions with negative consequences. At the heart of this theory is the concept of reinforcement. We say that a behaviour is positively reinforced when the consequences associated with it are positive and, as a result, the behaviour becomes more likely to be repeated. If, on the contrary, the consequences are negative, then the behaviour will be negatively reinforced.

One interesting application of instrumental conditioning is the concept of *shaping* (Rothschild and Gaidis, 1981). When the behaviour to be learned is complex, an effective strategy is to employ successive but varied reinforcing actions that will establish a gradual learning process. Suppose, for example, that a musical ensemble wants to increase attendance at its concerts by attracting a new clientèle. Going to the concert is a relatively complex behaviour. You need to buy the tickets, plan your schedule, decide on a mode of transportation, get to the venue, find your place in the hall, and so on. For many people who would like to attend concerts, these steps can represent significant obstacles which are likely to discourage them. The goal of shaping is to reinforce simple behaviours in a way that gradually leads to the learning of the targeted behaviour, which in our example is attending concerts. The organization could, for example, offer music lovers a significant discount on the price of a concert with, as a bonus, a metro ticket valid on the day of the event. When people arrive at the venue, they are welcomed by employees (or volunteers) who direct them to their designated seats. They are then given a coupon which entitles them to a smaller discount on the price of the next concert. The process is repeated with reinforcing incentives (e.g., price reductions) which gradually decrease until it is ultimately just the positive consequences of the behaviour itself (a nice evening at the concert hall) which serve as the reinforcement.

An important marketing phenomenon which is associated with classical conditioning is that of loyalty to the brand or organization. A consumer who is loyal to a brand not only prefers that brand to competing ones but has somehow made a personal commitment to always choose that brand, even though competing offers may sometimes seem more advantageous (Oliver, 1999). This commitment is presumably built on the foundation of positive past experiences of consumption (reinforcement). Consumers may be inclined to buy only one brand for a variety of reasons—availability, inertia, social pressure, and others—so this inclination alone does not mean they are loyal to that brand. To deduce whether or not someone is loyal to a brand, it is not enough to simply examine the purchases they make. It is also necessary to assess the extent to which the repeated purchase of a brand over time is part of the consumer's system of values and preferences—in other words, to understand the relationship which unites the consumer with this brand (Lichtlé and Plichon, 2008).

How cognitive theorists view learning

For cognitivists, one cannot discuss learning without reference to how the mind of a consumer processes the information reaching their senses—more specifically, how that information is acquired, stored, and retrieved from memory. Indeed, memory is at the root of every cognitive approach to learning.

A model of how the mind processes information is shown in Figure 4.2. This model distinguishes three types of memory: sensory, short-term, and long-term memory.

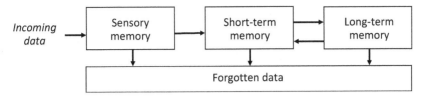

Figure 4.2 An Information processing model to explain and describe mental processes (d'Astous et al., 2018).

As the model shows, information about the environment is first captured by sensory memory. Most of this information is soon forgotten, but a selection is then processed by short-term memory. Again, much of this processed information is forgotten, but a selection is stored in long-term memory.

Sensory memory is visual or auditory. It can record a very large amount of information. But unless that information is processed more deeply, it will be retained for only a very short period of time. Some of the information recorded by sensory memory will be transferred to short-term memory, which can contain only a small number of distinct pieces of information (for most people, the number is between 5 and 9). Repeating this information internally—such as when you want to remember a phone number—makes it easier to transfer it to long-term memory. We can increase our memory capacity in the short term by grouping information into clearly separate elements. For example, most people process the three-digit area codes for telephone numbers as one block of information rather than three. Short-term memory is sometimes said to function as a work desk, a place where information from the outside (filtered by sensory memory) and from the inside (retrieved from long-term memory) is processed.

Long-term memory operates as the permanent archives for storing knowledge. Its capacity is very large, even unlimited. These memory archives can be separated into two types: semantic and episodic. Semantic memory consists of generic knowledge which, unlike the knowledge in episodic memory, is not linked to any specific context. For example, experienced classical music fans will know that

Mozart composed a number of piano concertos. They cannot associate this knowledge with a specific context, although constructing it must have occurred within one (reading a book, hearing a comment from a friend, buying a set of CDs, etc.); so, we can say the knowledge is part of their semantic memory. If tomorrow, for example, you are asked to explain the distinction between semantic memory and episodic memory, you will remember that you learned it by reading this chapter; this knowledge is part of your episodic memory. One day, no doubt, it will lose its contextual dimension and simply be stored with all the other knowledge of your semantic memory.

Associative memory networks

Our discussion of perception in the previous chapter referred to the concept of schema. We defined a schema as a mental structure or representation that includes knowledge, feelings, and images about an object. We emphasized the important role of schemata in the perception process: they control the selection of information from the environment, trigger the production of inferences, and simplify the retrieval of information from memory. The perceptual cycle (Neisser, 1976) is the model for how these different cognitive processes unfold.

Let us now look more deeply at what "mental structure" connotes. A widely accepted cognitive model in social sciences and marketing research is the *associative network*—or more specifically, what we may call a network model of associative memory (Wyer and Carlston, 1979). To illustrate, Figure 4.3 presents a hypothetical (and greatly simplified) example of such a network formed around the concept of "Pompidou Centre".

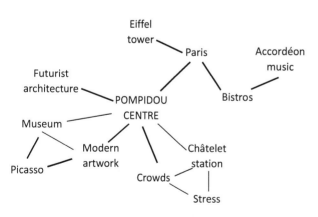

Figure 4.3 A hypothetical associative memory network.

The associative network is a useful way to imagine how long-term memory organizes information. In the example shown in Figure 4.3, associations between concepts—made through images, impressions, feelings, odours, or sounds—are represented by straight lines. We can see the Pompidou Centre is associated with Paris, with futuristic architecture, and with other concepts. Such associations are formed through experiences a person has undergone (say, during a trip to Paris), through information they have received (perhaps from a friend returning from a holiday in France), or through information they have gathered on their own (such as by consulting a website). The repeated linking of two concepts, in reality or in thought, is likely to increase the strength of their association. In Figure 4.3, stronger associations are represented by thicker lines.

The associative network provides an explanatory model for human thought. Thus, when a concept (e.g., Paris) is activated, the concepts associated with it (the Eiffel Tower, bistros) become active as well. This is called *spreading activation*. The closer the concepts and the stronger their association, the faster the activation will be. An interesting metaphor for understanding spreading activation is to imagine that the links travelling through the associative network are like different-sized pipes for circulating water.

According to the logic of spreading activation, one way to retrieve information stored in memory is to think of concepts associated with it. For example, a person who wishes to remember the name of a recently visited art gallery may activate in his mind an image of the place where the gallery is located. The more paths leading to a concept, the greater the likelihood that the concept will be activated, that is, that the desired information will be retrieved. From this observation comes a fundamental principle of learning: if we are to integrate new knowledge in our long-term memory, we must enrich that knowledge by combining it with other knowledge—this is known as *elaborative processing* or *elaboration*. For example, to remember the different concepts presented in this chapter, one can elaborate around them, create one's own examples, and build memorable images (like imagining the water flowing through the pipes).

How socialization theorists view learning

The behavioural and cognitive perspectives of learning are mainly limited to "snapshot" (cross-sectional) situations; the researchers attempt to explain how a given experience gives rise to learning. Yet, from the day we are born, each of us learns continuously. The concept of consumer socialization lets us see learning differently—with a diachronic or longitudinal view that considers how learning extends throughout life. More specifically, consumer socialization is defined as the process by which people acquire the skills, knowledge, and attitudes necessary for their development as consumers in a society (d'Astous et al., 2018, p. 143).

A useful way to model this process has been proposed by Moschis (1987). According to this researcher, a person's learning during his or her lifetime can be explained with the aid of three categories of variables: social structural variables, age or position in the lifecycle, and relationships with agents of socialization. Let us look briefly at each category.

Social structural variables

Would Wolfgang Amadeus Mozart have become "Mozart" if his father Leopold had been a doctor (or something else) rather than a composer, music teacher, and musician? If his father had been a doctor, Mozart might also have become a doctor in turn, and the world would never have known his genius for music. And who would need a Dr Mozart! This distressing idea shows how the social environment has a determining influence on the way people learn as they develop over time. The social environment is one of the social structural variables influencing how and what consumers learn all through their lives. Others such variables, like social class, gender, or ethnocultural origin, play a very important role in the construction of the self—in the development of our beliefs, attitudes, values, thought patterns, and decision-making.

Age or position in the lifecycle

Naturally, the learning we achieve during childhood is different from the learning achieved during adolescence and later in life. This results from the need to adapt to social environments as they change over the course of our lives. The young child's world revolves around his family; the adolescent's world is more influenced by friends (their peers); the adult's world is shaped by all the people and institutions that define life in society at large.

We should make two important observations in this regard. First, the capacities and modes of learning in consumers are not static; they evolve with the passage of time. Thus, children's cognitive skills—and their understanding of what consumption signifies, for example—are much less developed between the ages of 3 and 7 (at the perceptual stage) than between the ages of 7 and 11 (the analytical stage) and between the ages of 11 and 16 (the strategic stage; Roedder John, 1999). Second, learning is cumulative. Among other things, this means what we learn at one point in time is likely to contribute to what we learn at a later point. For example, consumers are more likely to develop an interest in theatre if they regularly attended plays during childhood.

Agents of socialization

Socialization is a learning process in which different agents of that process play a role. These agents are entities (individuals, institutions, groups) connected to a person via some form of socializing relationship, either formal (e.g., employer) or informal (e.g., family, friends). The influence of such agents on learning varies according to the position of the person in his or her life cycle. While family, peers, and school play a leading role in socializing children and adolescents, the media, friends, and colleagues have an influence that extends throughout the lifecycle.

Learning effected through agents of socialization takes place in three fundamental processes: modelling (learning by observing others), reinforcement (learning to behave in a way that leads to rewards and prevents punishments), and social interaction (learning to adapt to the social environment).

LEARNING IN THE FIELD OF ARTS AND CULTURE

Cultural transmission

Cultural sociologists and marketing researchers investigated the phenomenon of cultural democratization long before this concept appeared on the radar of managers in arts and culture organizations. In France, in 1979, the sociologist Pierre Bourdieu published a major work entitled *La distinction: Critique sociale du jugement*, which postulates the concept of "cultural capital" to express how an appreciation of sophisticated art forms (or "taste") can be transmitted between people, classes, or generations, just as economic capital can be transmitted.[1] Bourdieu argues that parents in the wealthiest and most educated classes endow their children with a taste for fine arts, whereas children in less fortunate socioeconomic classes do not regularly benefit from this kind of transmission. This cultural transmission also takes place in schools under the influence of teachers and through introductory classes in the arts (Kracman, 1996). Children who have received a musical education, for example, generally have a higher propensity to attend concerts when they are adults.

A legitimate question to be asked by anyone with a stake in cultural marketing: how does an interest in arts and culture take shape? Marketing researchers first attempted an answer with a survey-based study (Andreasen and Belk, 1980) which examined the following questions: how do preferences for theatre and classical music concerts develop? How much were consumers interested in classical music or theatre during their childhood and adolescence? How interested were their parents in these forms of art? The results of their study show that three elements play an important role in the development of preferences for sophisticated art: (1) their expectations, that is, to what degree consumers believe an evening at the theatre or a classical concert will be a positive experience; (2) their attitudes and lifestyle vis-à-vis the consumption of arts and culture (e.g., are they cultural enthusiasts who fervently dedicate themselves to activities like these?); and (3) their exposure to artistic interests when they were young—especially the degree to which their parents were a vector of cultural transmission.

Many studies have investigated these questions further since Andreasen and Belk published their pioneering research. We now know that cultural transmission is a complex phenomenon with its starting point in childhood. This does not mean that a person cannot discover an interest in theatre or fine arts in adulthood; a new spouse or a new circle of friends, for example, can lead someone to be interested in theatre or museums (Gainer, 1995). Rather, it seems the formation of an interest in these activities is facilitated when a person is exposed to widely acclaimed works of art as early in life as possible. Acquiring an interest in arts and culture through parental influence does not apply uniquely to domestic cultural products. It also encompasses foreign products, especially in film and music.

Although the values transmitted by parents constitute a powerful phenomenon of cultural transmission (Gainer, 1997), the immediate family is not the only agent of cultural socialization. Children may be initiated into appreciating art by members of their extended family, be they uncles, aunts, grandparents, or cousins. This learning may be developed and reinforced further at school, by teachers who are passionate about art and by peers who inspire youth people to adopt an artistic pursuit or interest (Carù and Cova, 2011). Studies have shown, however, that early cultural socialization within the family exerts a more powerful influence than the school (Aschaffenburg and Maas, 1997; Kraaykamp, 2003; Nagel et al., 2010). The taste for reading is a special case; it can be acquired both within the family and in school (Meuleman et al., 2018). The taste for sophisticated art, however, usually develops through interaction with one or several agents of socialization—family, school, or circles of friends.

In addition to the influence of family, school, or peers, the act of attending a show or visiting a museum when we are young, regardless of the context in which such experiences occur, is another important learning factor in this journey. People who attended shows or visited museums with their parents when they were young are 1.6 times more likely to be interested in them in adulthood (Octobre et al., 2010).

Likewise, the birth of a career in the arts is usually instigated by one of these influences or by a combination (Charland-Lallier and Colbert, 2017). Note, however, that this potential for influence diminishes as the child grows older. Socialization appears to be less effective during adolescence (Meuleman et al., 2018). Dutch researchers have studied the influence of high school arts classes on future participation by students in cultural activities (Nagel et al., 2010). They concluded there is no difference in future levels of participation between those who took the classes and those who did not. Their results even suggest that interest in attending such classes at the high school level or in participating in cultural outings is conditioned beforehand by socialization to art within the family or at primary school.

Last, given the importance of social media in the lives of young consumers, it is not surprising to learn that cultural transmission is commonly effected via social media (Hausmann, 2012). Unlike the phenomenon of conventional word-of-mouth (from person to person), which may reach just a dozen people or so in a given circle of acquaintance, social media word-of-mouth often enables hundreds of people to be contacted (Hausmann, 2012).

The importance of the past

While socialization to arts and culture has a greater potential influence at the beginning of a person's lifecycle, other moments in life are also important. For example, studies have shown that later in life, people generally prefer the same popular music they listened to in adolescence or early adulthood (Holbrook and Schindler, 1989). It appears our taste for popular music crystallizes when we are in transition from adolescence to the adult world. A preference for the music we loved in our 20s also resonates with some consumers as an aesthetic preference rooted in the past. Researchers describe it as a *nostalgia effect* (Holbrook and Schindler, 1994; Zimprich and Wolf, 2016). For both women and men, there is a market segment for cultural products that recall their past. This preference is associated with the strong emotions we experience during a certain time of life. For some people, this return to the past entails a sense of loss from a period of life perceived as better. For others, it may be a reminder of happy or melancholy memories, or a revival of an aesthetic preference acquired in their youth.

Gendered learning

In every survey profiling the clients of arts and culture organizations, the audiences are shown to have a higher proportion of female members than male. Women attend more performing arts centres and museums, read more novels, and in general have a greater curiosity for artistic events and activities. Several studies have shown the explanation for this phenomenon lies in the values which parents transmit to their children from a very early age (Gainer, 1993). The situation can be summarized by the following cliché: "Sport is for boys, and art is for girls". Although one might think this type of gender-based behaviour no longer applies to the 21st century, recent publications show that arts and culture audiences are still composed mostly of women. This majority fluctuates depending on the type of art (Christin, 2012). The explanation remains, still today, that parents are gendering the socialization of their children. Moreover, gendered socialization seems to be amplified by the fact that women are predominant in occupations related to arts and culture. Working for a cultural organization may lead these women to attend more artistic and cultural events than the women working in other sectors of the economy (Christin, 2012).

One interesting study showed the participation of boys and girls in arts and culture in American high schools is different depending on the environment where the school is located. For example, the gap in positive participation between girls and boys is even greater in rural schools. It appears that the rural sociological context—more traditional roles for boys and girls—is reflected in greater participation by girls in extracurricular arts activities (Schmutz et al., 2016).

Learning not to like

A frequent subject for discussion in the cultural field is the role of nonparticipants, meaning those who are not interested in the arts at all. Here, it is important to fully understand the purpose of this questioning. In general, *nonparticipant* means someone who does not attend events which fall into the category of sophisticated or "high-brow" forms of art. It is important to be precise because when we consult statistics on cultural consumption and combine the consumption of artistic works from both the sophisticated and the popular arts, we see that almost everyone in the population consumes a great deal of cultural products. If we add up purchasing cinema tickets, reading novels, watching television series (both on traditional broadcast or cable channels and on web-streaming services like Netflix), in addition to attending performing arts centres, festivals, and museums of all kinds, the evidence is unmistakable: the "nonparticipant" in culture is an illusion. On the other hand, from our discussion in previous sections, we know that learning to appreciate sophisticated art forms is more likely to be effective if it happens at an early age. And, contrary to what one might assume, the nonparticipant in sophisticated art is not someone who is unaware of what sophisticated arts are. Nonparticipants know very well why they are not interested in so-called sophisticated art (Barret, 2009; Stevenson, 2019). So, their lack of consumption in this area is not based on a lack of awareness, but on a fully conscious and reason-based decision. Socialization, in their case, has produced a contrary effect. Ultimately, it appears the factors involved in participation or nonparticipation are partly linked to individual tastes and preferences—for example, some are passionate about wrestling, while others see no interest in it—and, for nonparticipants, to very down-to-earth concerns about the way of dressing, the strange conventions and rituals to be followed, or the content of what is presented (e.g., "this is not for me, I do not pretend to be someone I am not").

IMPLICATIONS FOR THE MARKETING OF ARTS AND CULTURE

What should we retain as the implications of this knowledge in terms of what promotes learning and appreciation of sophisticated art forms? First, shows intended for young audiences, along with similar initiatives by orchestras or museums, help create future generations of art lovers. A fun and interesting artistic or cultural experience with a parent promotes learning, and repeating the experience will act as a reinforcement (instrumental conditioning). The enjoyment of visiting an exhibition or listening to a concert activates a sensory memory, which will later be stored in long-term memory, especially if the moment is "magical", and this positive experience is repeated. Over time, an associative memory network will form around the components of the overall consumption experience: venue, atmosphere, complementary activities (e.g., going to the restaurant before or after the event), emotions felt, names of works and artists, and so on. When subsequently activated in the mind, each component can contribute, via the phenomenon of spreading activation, to reviving the lived experience in the present. It is therefore important that artistic and cultural organizations implement strategies for enriching and solidifying the child's associative network during the consumer experience, because this will increase their ability to recall the associated benefits in the future. There are many examples: bring children on a theatre stage to show them the sets; let them meet the actors; encourage them to try the musical instruments; introduce them to painting; or show them how an artist works in the studio. A parent who values reading or art in general makes a strong impression on a child, in the same way that a passionate art teacher can transmit a love of art to their students.

But what about people whose families are less fortunate economically, or those who do not show an interest in arts and culture and do not attend theatres and museums? Perhaps the technique of shaping we outlined earlier could prove useful in encouraging them to gradually form an appreciation of sophisticated art. However, we must remain aware of the barriers that exist for them as potential consumers. For some it will be the cost of the ticket. For others, a false perception of the prerequisites for attending a concert: "I wouldn't know what to wear"; "I don't know how to behave during a concert"; "classical music is not for uneducated people like me". Different people will have different reasons. If there is a total lack of interest in or taste for this type of consumption, it may be impossible to change their habits. The cold truth may simply be that some groups of potential consumers cannot be persuaded even with a great investment of time, energy, and money.

That being said, and on a more optimistic note, if the goal is simply to give an opportunity for a nonparticipant to come into contact with a form of art, there are ways to achieve that goal. For example, cultural managers can organize isolated events such as free outdoor classical concerts. Group outings to such events often include people from outside the core group of art lovers, so there is a chance to spark their interest and draw them into the circle of appreciation. One must remember that spending an evening at the theatre or visiting a museum is both an aesthetic and a social experience; people usually go in the company of at least one other person (Debenedetti, 2003). This social experience is as important as the art form itself. It remains important, however, to identify the root reasons for a lack of interest in consuming arts and culture, and to find ways to transplant such an interest. Simply reducing the price of tickets may not be sufficient.

IMPLICATIONS FOR RESEARCH

As we have seen in this chapter, socialization is a central focus for much of the research on learning as it relates to arts and culture consumption. We should expect it to be so, since this type of consumption is not standard among consumers—in the case of the sophisticated arts, at least. Researchers in the field are therefore inclined to study the fundamental factors which explain why some consumers have an interest in arts and culture and others do not. Because the business environment is the same overall for consumers in general (e.g., museums exist, they are there for everyone), the eyes of researchers have naturally turned to examining the socialization process. The results of their research confirm the important role played by the socialization agents—family and school, most of all—in developing cultural preferences.

We would argue, however, that to draw a more complete picture of this important theme, other learning aspects deserve further study. We have alluded, for example, to the fact that consuming arts and culture is a complex activity for anyone who has not assimilated the many patterns associated with it. Gradual learning (shaping), through the use of successive steps of reinforcement, can be an interesting way to acquire the knowledge necessary to become a regular consumer of arts and culture. To explore this idea, studies based on the "action research" approach should be conducted.

Classical conditioning also offers an interesting research path, particularly with respect to the various partnerships that cultural organizations are putting forward to build their brand. One thinks here of the sponsorship programmes which are primarily designed to support arts and culture activities financially, but whose influence on consumer reactions and on the associations generated in their minds is still unknown (see Colbert et al., 2005). Similarly, the use of celebrities as spokespeople to promote arts and culture institutions or cultural activities is a virtually blank area of research, despite the very significant corpus of marketing literature which exists in this field. Several interesting research tracks which can be adapted to the context of arts and culture have been proposed by Bergkvist and Zhou (2016); for example, how should a cultural organization choose a spokesperson, and how should an advertising or public relations campaign involving a spokesperson be managed?

Last, we know little about what cultural consumers retain in their long-term memory from experiences such as visiting a museum, attending a play, or taking part in a festival, or about the effects of these memory traces on their future behaviours. To what extent, for example, does the act of stimulating the elaboration of memory through artistic or cultural content enrich the mental representations of such content and, possibly, contribute to the formation of positive expectations for future consumer experiences? What is the effect of these richer mental representations on interest in arts and culture in general and on the desire to share this interest with others? Does the elaboration of associative memory networks around artistic and cultural experiences allow consumers to diversify the spectrum of activities they consume? These are just a few of the many relevant research questions which emerge from the intersection of learning and cultural marketing.

Note

1   First published in English as *Distinction: A Social Critique of the Judgement of Taste* (1984), Cambridge, MA: Harvard University Press.

REFERENCES

Andreasen, A. R. and R. W. Belk (1980), "Predictors of Attendance at the Performing Arts", *Journal of Consumer Research*, 7 (2), 112–220.

Aschaffenburg, K. and I. Maas (1997), "Cultural and Educational Careers: The Dynamics of Social Reproduction", *American Sociological Review*, 62 (4), 573–587.

Barret, M. (2009), "Exploring 'Class' in the Field of Theatregoing", unpublished doctoral thesis, University of Warwick Centre for Cultural Policy Studies, Warwick.

Bergkvist, L. and K. Q. Zhou (2016), "Celebrity Endorsements: A Literature Review and Research Agenda", *International Journal of Advertising*, 35 (4), 642–663.

Bourdieu, P. (1979). *La distinction: Critique sociale du jugement*, Paris: Les Éditions de Minuit.

Carù, A. and B. Cova (2011), "Can the Generation Gap Impede Immersion in an Exhibition? The Case of Annisettanta (The 1970s)", *International Journal of Arts Management*, 13 (2), 16–28.

Charland-Lallier, M. and F. Colbert (2017), "Factors Influencing the Choice of a Career Path in the Arts", *American Journal of Arts Management* (online journal), January 2017.

Christin, A. (2012), "Gender and Highbrow Cultural Participation in the United Sates", *Poetics*, 40 (5), 423–443.

Colbert, F., A. d'Astous, and M.-A. Parmentier (2005), "Consumer Perception of Private versus Public Sponsorship of the Arts", *International Journal of Arts Management*, 8 (1), 48–60.

Colbert, F. et al. (2018), *Marketing Culture and the Arts*, 5th edition, Montréal: Carmelle and Rémi-Marcoux Chair in Arts Management, HEC Montréal.

d'Astous, A., N. Daghfous, P. Balloffet, and C. Boulaire (2018), *Comportement du consommateur*, 5th edition, Montréal: Chenelière Éducation.

Debenedetti, S. (2003), "Investigating the Role of Companions in the Art Museum Experience", *International Journal of Arts Management*, 5 (3), 52–63.

Gainer, B. (1993), "The Importance of Gender to Arts Marketing", *Journal of Arts Management, Law and Society*, 23 (3), 240–252.

Gainer, B. (1995), "Rituals and Relationships: Interpersonal Influences on Shared Consumption", *Journal of Business Research*, 32 (3), 253–260.

Gainer, B. (1997), "Marketing Arts Education: Parental Attitudes towards Arts Education for Children", *Journal of Arts Management, Law and Society*, 26 (4), 253–268.

Hausmann, A. (2012), "The Importance of Word of Mouth for Museums: An Analytical Framework", *International Journal of Arts Management*, 14 (3), 32–43.

Holbrook, M. B. and R. M. Schindler (1989), "Some Explanatory Findings on the Development of Musical Tastes", *Journal of Consumer Research*, 16 (1), 119–124.

Holbrook, M. B. and R. M. Schindler (1994), "Age, Sex and Attitude toward the Past as Predictors of Consumers' Aesthetic Tastes for Cultural Products", *Journal of Marketing Research*, 31 (3), 412–422.

Kracman, K. (1996), "The Effect of School-Based Arts Instruction on Attendance at Museums and the Performing Arts", *Poetics*, 24 (2–4), 203–218.

Kraaykamp, G. (2003), "Literary Socialization and Reading Preferences: Effects of Parents, the Library, and the School", *Poetics*, 31, 235–257.

Lichtlé, M.-C. and V. Plichon (2008), "Mieux comprendre la fidélité des consommateurs", *Recherche et Applications en Marketing*, 23 (4), 121–141.

Meuleman, R., M. Lubbers, and M. Ver (2018), "Parental Socialization and the Consumption of Domestic Films, Books and Music", *Journal of Consumer Culture*, 18 (1), 103–130.

Moschis, G. P. (1987), *Consumer Socialization*, Lexington, KY: D.C. Heath.

Nagel, I., M-L. Damen, and F. Haanstra (2010), "The Arts Course CKV1 and Cultural Participation in the Netherlands", *Poetics*, 38 (4), 365–385.

Neisser, U. (1976), *Cognition and Reality*, San Francisco, CA: Freeman.

Octobre, S., C. Détrez, P. Mercklé, and Berthomier (2010), *L'enfance des loisirs*, Paris: Ministère de la Culture et de la Communication.

Oliver, R. L. (1999), "Whence Consumer Loyalty?", *Journal of Marketing*, 63, 33–44.

Roedder John, D. (1999), "Consumer Socialization of Children: A Retrospective Look at Twenty-Five Years of Research", *Journal of Consumer Research*, 26 (3), 183–213.

Rothschild, M. L. and W. C. Gaidis (1981), "Behavioral Learning Theory: Its Relevance to Marketing and Promotion", *Journal of Marketing*, 45 (2), 70–78.

Schmutz, V., E. Stearns, and E. J. Glennie (2016), "Cultural Capital Formation in Adolescence: High Schools and the Gender Gap in Arts Activity Participation", *Poetics*, 57 (4), 27–39.

Stevenson, D. (2019), "The Cultural Non-Participant: Critical Logics and Discursive Subject Identities", *Arts and the Market*, 9 (1), 50–64.

Wyer, R. S. Jr. and D. E. Carlston (1979), *Social Cognition, Inference, and Attribution*, New York, NY: Erlbaum.

Zimprich, D. and T. Wolf (2016), "The Distribution of Memories for Popular Songs in Old Age: An Individual Differences Approach", *Psychology of Music*, 44 (4), 640–657.

Attitudes and affective states
Chapter 5

In Chapters 3 and 4, we saw that consumer experiences are constructed and lived on the basis of knowledge and memories which are acquired through perception, either previously or immediately. Our discussion focused primarily on the cognitive aspects of experience—beliefs, judgements, and opinions.
In this chapter, we will look at the consumption experience from a different and complementary angle and examine the *affect* of consumers, by which we mean their affective states (feelings, emotions, moods) and their attitudes. As a first step, we will summarize the knowledge which consumer behaviour researchers have compiled on these themes in recent decades. Subsequently, we will examine the results of research studies on these themes in the field of arts and culture. In the last two sections of this chapter, we discuss the practical implications of those results and suggest new relevant avenues for future research.

CONSUMERS LIVE AFFECTIVE EXPERIENCES

Attitudes

A generally accepted definition of *attitude* is the following: "A learned predisposition to respond in a consistently favorable or unfavorable manner with respect to a given object" (Fishbein and Ajzen, 1975, p. 6). To illustrate, let us consider a person's attitude towards Cirque du Soleil. This definition implies two things: this attitude has been constructed over time (i.e., it has been learned), and it can be positive or negative to varying degrees. An attitude is a mental representation, a psychological concept—it is not directly observable. But one can discern its nature by examining how people behave in relation to the object of their attitude or, better still, by listening to what they have to say about it.

Perform the following test. Ask someone what they think of a specific object they know, such as a musical ensemble or theatre troupe. Let them speak freely as you listen. In general, their remarks should include three types of information: (1) comments referring to beliefs (e.g., "These musicians have great talent"); (2) comments containing an evaluation ("I like most of the actors in this troupe"); and (3) comments that refer to behaviours or intentions ("I plan to renew my membership"). For some researchers in psychology and consumer behaviour, these three types of remarks represent the three basic components of attitudes: the cognitive component (beliefs), the affective component (evaluations or feelings), and the conative component (intentions or behaviours). This is known as the tripartite model of attitudes or the three-dimensional perspective.

However, the vast majority of researchers in the social sciences have abandoned the three-dimensional perspective of attitudes in favour of the one-dimensional perspective, that is, a conception where attitude corresponds only to the affective component (evaluations and feelings) and where the three components are not only conceptually distinct but causally linked together, as shown in Figure 5.1.

The researcher who did the most to advance the one-dimensional perspective of attitudes is undoubtedly the psychologist Martin Fishbein. In 1963, he proposed a behaviourist theory regarding the formation of attitudes which had considerable influence on research and practice in many social science disciplines, including marketing.

According to Fishbein (1963), an attitude is determined by a relatively small number (between 5 and 9) of beliefs which are "salient". Although one can have several different beliefs

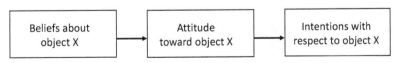

Figure 5.1 The one-dimensional perspective (d'Astous et al., 2018).

about an object, Fishbein (1963) argues that only those which are salient actually contribute to the formation of an attitude. In general, a belief corresponds to the probability that the attitude object has a given attribute (e.g., the probability that a musical ensemble contains highly talented musicians). It is therefore common to refer to salient beliefs or salient attributes. Salient beliefs about a given object often vary from person to person; identifying them is an empirical process, commonly achieved through spontaneous activation (e.g., "say all the things which come to mind when you think of Cirque du Soleil").

Fishbein's multi-attribute model

One can explain the great popularity of the one-dimensional conception of attitudes among researchers by the fact that its author has associated it with an algebraic model aimed at making it operational. This model, called the multi-attribute model of attitudes, takes the following form:

$$A_o = \sum_{i=1}^{n} b_i e_i$$

In this equation, A_o stands for the attitude towards object o, while b_i is the strength of the belief that object o has the attribute i, and e_i is the evaluation of attribute i. Last, n stands for the number of salient attributes (or salient beliefs). According to this model, an attitude corresponds to the sum of the products of beliefs and evaluations relating to a set n of salient attributes. The right side of the equation is commonly referred to as the cognitive structure of the attitude.

Fishbein (1963) attached strict measurement requirements to this model. For example, the beliefs (b_i) and the evaluations (e_i) must be measured using symmetric bipolar numerical scales with boundaries marked by negative scores (low probability, negative evaluation) and by positive scores (high probability, positive evaluation). As an illustration, suppose a salient attribute in the formation of an attitude towards Cirque du Soleil were to be "delivers circus shows that include feats of acrobatic prowess". Appropriate measures of belief and evaluation relative to this attribute would be as follows:

Belief (*b*):

Cirque du Soleil delivers circus shows that include feats of acrobatic prowess:

Unlikely   −3 : −2 : −1 : 0 : +1 : +2 : +3 :   Likely

Evaluation (*e*):

Producing shows that include feats of acrobatic prowess is:

Bad   −3 : −2 : −1 : 0 : +1 : +2 : +3 :   Good

The reader will no doubt have noted that multiplying two negative scores results in a positive number; therefore, the relative absence of a negatively valued attribute contributes positively to the attitude. Other outcomes (two positive scores, one positive score, and one negative score) also agree with this attitudinal logic.

Table 5.1 presents a fictitious numerical example of the cognitive structure of two consumers in the context of the formation of their attitude towards Cirque du Soleil. For the purposes of this example, it is assumed that the five attributes selected are salient.

In addition to showing the algebraic mechanics of the multi-attribute model, this numerical example emphasizes that different cognitive structures can give rise to the same attitude score (here, +5). Thus, we see the first consumer especially

Table 5.1 Two fictitious cognitive structures (attitude towards Cirque du Soleil)

Attribute	Consumer 1 b_i	e_i	$b_i e_i$	Consumer 2 b_i	e_i	$b_i e_i$
Acrobatic feats	+3	+3	+9	+3	−2	−6
Degree of exoticism	+2	+2	+4	+1	+2	+2
Originality of the music	−2	+1	−2	+3	+3	+9
Performance by the actors	+1	0	0	+1	−3	−3
Link to nature	+3	−2	−6	+1	+3	+3
Total			+5			+5

likes exoticism and acrobatics and strongly believes Cirque du Soleil delivers them. The second consumer, however, does not appreciate the feats by the acrobats or the performances by the actors; she prefers the exotic aspect of the shows, their connection with nature, and the originality of the music, and perceives that the performance of Cirque du Soleil in terms of this latter attribute is very high in quality.

Strategic implications

An important marketing objective for any company is to ensure its products and brands are not only evaluated favourably by consumers but are also evaluated *more* favourably than the ones offered by competitors. We can derive useful strategies for achieving this goal from the multi-attribute model. To make consumer attitudes towards a brand more favourable, we can (1) attempt to improve the brand's position on attributes evaluated positively or reduce the position on those evaluated negatively (strategies focusing on beliefs); (2) attempt to increase the evaluation of attributes where the brand is well positioned or reduce the evaluation where it is poorly positioned (strategies focusing on evaluations); (3) introduce a new attribute where the brand is well perceived and make it salient; and (4) attempt to influence consumers' opinion of competing brands (e.g., suggest the competing brand is less well positioned on a positively valued attribute).

These various strategies for making consumer attitudes more favourable will not be new to experienced marketing managers. What makes them interesting is the fact that they derive from a generally accepted theory of consumer attitude formation. In addition, the algebraic model associated with this theory provides an operational structure enabling rigorous monitoring of their effectiveness.

A critical look

The vision proposed by the multi-attribute model to explain the formation of attitudes is fundamentally analytical. Most researchers in marketing and the humanities believe attitudes are not always created from beliefs. For example, striking or shocking images (e.g., plastic waste strewn across a beach) can also directly give rise to strong attitudes (e.g., attitude towards elimination of pollution). Also, as we saw in Chapter 4, the categorization of an object generally involves the transfer of meanings from the mental category—including its affective qualities—to the object. For example, a new show (the object) by Cirque du Soleil (the category) is sure to be evaluated favourably by a fan of the Cirque, without mobilizing any of their beliefs. The simple fact of attending a performance somewhere pleasant or loaded with positive symbols (Carnegie Hall, for example) is likely to influence anyone's evaluation of that performance.

Although strategically useful, the vision proposed by Fishbein (1963) appears limiting in that it focuses solely on the analysis of cognitive information (beliefs). Elements in the periphery or environment of an object (odours, music, people, etc.) can play an important role in shaping our attitude towards it, sometimes even unconsciously. In the end, it must be recognized that attitudes are formed from many kinds of information, not just from cognitive data (see Zanna and Rempel, 1988).

A relevant extension

The value of attitude as a concept lies mainly in its presumed ability to predict behaviour. A person who has a positive attitude towards an object should, in principle, behave positively with respect to that object (e.g., if it is a product, to speak positively about, or to buy it). Yet many studies have shown that, for diverse reasons, the relationship between attitude and behaviour is not always strong (Fishbein and Ajzen, 2010). Fishbein (e.g., Fishbein and Ajzen, 1975) argues that a logical way to predict a behavioural intention is to consider the attitude towards this behaviour. For example, a positive attitude towards the act of attending a Cirque du Soleil show is more predictive of an intention to do so than a positive attitude towards the Cirque per se.

Fishbein proposed an extension of the multi-attribute model in cases where the attitude object is a behaviour. The model is as follows:

$$A_b = \sum_{i=1}^{n} b_i e_i$$

In this equation, A_b stands for the attitude towards behaviour b, while b_i is the strength of the belief that behaviour b will give rise to consequence i, and e_i is the evaluation of consequence i. Last, n is the number of salient beliefs. As we can see, the structure of this model resembles that of the multi-attribute model presented earlier. Its application therefore follows the same logic. The main difference is that the salient beliefs associated with this model refer to consequences rather than to attributes. This model is called the *theory of reasoned action* (TRA or ToRA: Fishbein and Ajzen, 1975). A more elaborate conception of it, called the *reasoned action approach* (RAA) takes into account the social pressures exerted by the environment and the degree to which the person is able to accomplish the behaviour (resources, skills, constraints). This variant was developed by Fishbein and Ajzen (2010); for an application in the arts domain, see d'Astous et al. (2005).

Affective states

The concept of attitude is not sufficient to fully describe the affective reactions people experience when acting as consumers. For example, two consumers with a comparable attitude towards a theatrical performance will not necessarily undergo a similar psychological experience (be it of pain, joy, euphoria, or other emotions). Accordingly, any discussion of consumer affect must also consider the role of affective states or, more precisely, the role of emotions and mood.

Emotions

Emotions are affective states which may be more or less enduring, more or less intense; they normally result from interaction with an object (in a broad sense). For example, one of the authors of this book once found himself in an airport waiting lounge furnished with a piano. Listening to the wrong notes produced by unskilled pianists who were a little too eager to display their technique in public, he felt irritated and frustrated at having to endure this racket, and expressed his dissatisfaction to the friends accompanying him. Irritation, frustration, and discontent are unpleasant negative emotions. Like other emotions, these are subjective experiences accompanied by physiological reactions (e.g., increased blood pressure), expressive reactions (raising your eyes to the sky), adaptive behaviours (directing your attention to something else), and cognitive responses ("well, this is just temporary, I will board the plane soon"). We can observe these various types of psychological events in the case of a large number of emotions, although it is difficult to establish their importance and even their necessity (Bagozzi et al., 1999).

Much of the research on emotions, in both psychology and marketing, has focused on establishing typologies for classifying emotions and on approaches to measuring them. Among the typologies of emotion which have been advanced for studying the consumption experience, that of Richins (1997) is the most general, since it aims to be relevant to all activities related to consumption. This typology, shown in Table 5.2, relies on what Richins (1997) calls *consumption emotion descriptors* (e.g., anger), each containing a set of indicators (frustrated, angry, irritated, etc.) used for measurement purposes. As we might suspect, the emotion descriptors of the Richins typology do not apply to all possible consumption situations. It behoves researchers to select the ones which appear most useful, given the object of their study.

The dimensional approach is a different way of addressing the problem of how to classify the full spectrum of human emotion. Advanced by the psychologists Mehrabian and Russell

Table 5.2 The Richins typology of emotions

Love (loving, sentimental, warm-hearted, compassionate)	*Joy* (happy, pleased, joyful, glad, delighted, cheerful)
Romantic love (sexy, romantic, passionate)	*Discontent* (unfulfilled, discontented)
Anger (frustrated, angry, irritated, aggravated, upset, furious)	*Optimism* (optimistic, encouraged, hopeful)
Contentment (contented, fulfilled)	*Peacefulness* (calm, peaceful)
Envy (envious, jealous)	*Fear* (scared, panicky, threatened)
Excitement (excited, enthusiastic)	*Loneliness* (lonely, homesick)
Shame (embarrassed, confused, ashamed, humiliated, offended)	*Surprise* (surprised, amazed, astonished)
Worry (nervous, worried, tense, anxious, concerned)	*Sadness* (depressed, sad, miserable,)
	Other items (guilty, proud, relieved, eager)

(1974), this approach involves using statistical techniques to define emotions according to fundamental dimensions. These two researchers proposed a taxonomy of emotion based on the intersection of two dimensions: one related to pleasure (unpleasant/pleasant) and the other to degree of stimulation (weak/strong). This intersection allows us to position many different affective states: the "unpleasant/weak stimulation" quadrant: sadness, depression, lethargy, fatigue; the "unpleasant/strong stimulation" quadrant: nervousness, stress, annoyance, tension; the "pleasant/weak stimulation" quadrant: calm, relaxation, serenity, contentment; the "pleasant/strong stimulation" quadrant: excitement, surprise, euphoria, joy, alertness.

Terms which qualify emotions are usually used to discover whether certain emotions were felt. For example, a researcher interested in measuring the excitement generated by a Cirque du Soleil show could use the following scales, defined from the indicators proposed by Richins (1997)—

during this Cirque du Soleil show, I felt:

Excited:

        Not at all   1 : 2 : 3 : 4 : 5 : 6 : 7 :   Greatly

Enthusiastic:

        Not at all   1 : 2 : 3 : 4 : 5 : 6 : 7 :   Greatly

In the example above, the researcher obtains a measurement of emotions through questioning. Other measurement methods can be used, such as examining facial expressions (see, for example, Derbaix, 1995) or measuring physiological variables such as brain waves, blood pressure, skin resistance, or heartbeat (see, for example, Wang and Minor, 2008). Survey-type questioning, however, remains the preferred approach for the majority of marketing researchers.

Mood

Unlike emotions, mood is an affective state which is less intense, more enduring, and not necessarily focused on a specific object (Bagozzi et al., 1999). Some researchers regard mood as an affective concept within an associative memory network (Bower, 1981; see also Chapter 4). For example, if a person is in a positive mood when visiting an art exhibition, the act of remembering that visit later will likely activate, through the process of spreading activation (see Chapter 4), the same positive mood.

A large number of studies in psychology and marketing have shown that mood has significant effects on information processing and behaviour (Isen, 1984). This research focuses mainly on positive mood, where the observed effects are more systematic. In general, it appears a positive mood leads to greater open-mindedness, which results in a tendency to be more sociable, more open to helping others, less analytical and more flexible when decisions are to be made, and more inclined to see the good side of things (Isen, 2008). The effects of a negative mood are sometimes contrasted with those associated with positive mood (e.g., being less open to helping others). These effects, however, are less generalizable. According to several researchers, we can ascribe this to the natural inclination of people who are in a bad mood to implement mood rehabilitation strategies (e.g., thinking about positive things).

AFFECTIVE EXPERIENCES IN THE FIELD OF ARTS AND CULTURE

In the previous sections, we discussed the concepts of attitude and affective states, specifically emotions and mood. Common consumer goods can elicit emotions from consumers, such as pleasure or satisfaction. In general, though, their function is mainly utilitarian; they are not expected to move us to tears or make us laugh. In contrast, the essence of an artistic product is to provoke emotions of many different kinds. In human beings, a work of art appeals as much to the mind as to the heart; it encourages symbolic, hedonic, and aesthetic motivations to consumption. As we have already mentioned, attending a show or visiting a museum is an experiential activity. The cultural product is an experiential product, just like other products in the service economy, except that art does not generally have the practical functions which underlie purchased services such as dining at a restaurant (to feed oneself) or flying on a passenger jet (to travel abroad).

When consumers attend a show or visit a museum, we say they are co-creators and co-producers of their experience—because, in doing so, they give meaning to what they see or hear, based on who they are or what they know (they co-produce), and they assign a value to what they have co-produced (co-creation). This co-production and co-creation process is influenced by their tastes and preferences, by their degree of preparation and knowledge regarding the art form in question, and by the quality of learning they have enjoyed in life and, more specifically, during their childhood (see Chapter 4). The process involves three actors: (1) the artist who proposes their unique vision of the world, (2) the consumer who gives meaning to what they see from their "nest" (to recall the analogy used in Chapter 3 for the process of appropriation), and (3) the cultural organization which presents the work in a specific physical context (the theatre, the museum, etc.) and can contribute by its actions to facilitating the process. Each of these three players brings a specific colour to the consumer experience. Moreover, this co-production and co-creation process draws simultaneously from the affect, cognition, and imagination of the spectator. The more familiar a person is with the type of art presented, the richer the experience will be, and the more valuable it will be in their eyes (Chan, 2019).

But as for co-producing such experiences (Minkiewicz et al., 2014)—how exactly does that occur? We can do it alone when observing the artwork before us, or by discussing it with others; we can co-produce our experience in a museum by choosing our own pathway through the exhibits, by assembling the specific components into our own "set", and by lingering on the works that speak to us the most—in other words, we can customize the experience. A consumer who is more familiar with an art form will be less disoriented by what they see and can spend more time giving meaning to the experience, thus making it richer and more emotionally rewarding. Their immersion in the experience may be deeper and more significant. External factors related to the quality of the service or to the presence of other people may disrupt the co-creation process, however, by generating interference. A museum which is packed with visitors, or staffed by careless employees, can have a negative impact, inhibit the co-production process, reduce co-creation of value, and ultimately give rise to negative emotions and attitudes (Minkiewicz et al., 2016).

Let's take a closer look at the components which form the experience of consuming a theatre show or museum visit. As we mentioned earlier, there are three such components: the artwork itself, the services offered by the venue, and the other spectators or participants (see Baker, 1986, for a similar typology associated with the service environment in general). The consumer experience giving rise to co-production and co-creation starts with the artist and their work and is deployed through the process of appropriation (see Chapter 3). The work itself provokes emotions in the spectator, who will find them more or less rewarding, as the case may be. Moreover, the majority of art consumption experiences do not take place in a vacuum. The venue where the spectator or visitor undergoes the experience is not a neutral component. It will be pleasant or not, and welcoming or not; it will influence the consumption experience by generating evaluations and emotions. No one is insensitive to the physical environment of a concert hall or museum. Architecture, decor, colours, comfort, cleanliness, and odours are elements which influence our evaluation of the overall experience and can significantly affect our degree of satisfaction. The quality of customer service can also have a significant effect on this experience. Courteous and efficient service by employees who show pleasure in welcoming spectators or visitors predisposes a person to hear what the artist is trying to say. Poor customer service, on the other hand, may provoke a bad mood and spoil the artistic experience (Colbert and Dantas, 2019; Obaidalahe et al., 2017).

The third element of the consumer experience concerns the social environment: the other participants and especially those who accompany the principal consumer. Studies of the clientèle attending arts and culture venues or events show the vast majority of spectators or visitors do not come alone; they are accompanied by romantic partners, children, friends, or fellow members of a group (Debenedetti, 2003). These accompanying spectators do not have a passive role. Their presence can be used to create or maintain emotional or social ties; they may enrich each other's experience through discussion; they may serve as a source of information, support, or encouragement when a difficult work of art disrupts the consumer or plunges them into unknown territory (negative emotions); or their influence may simply involve the pleasure of being among friends or family (Gainer, 1995). Ultimately, the accompanying people contribute to the consumption experience by creating feelings of well-being or pleasure. The behaviours of other participants also influence the consumption experience, either positively or negatively. Laughing alone in a half-empty hall is not the same thing as laughing in unison with 500 people. Similarly, a crowd may annoy us when it includes people making noise or behaving rudely.

In a nutshell, the experience of attending a show or visiting a museum consists of three interrelated elements which can influence (either positively or negatively) the attitudes, emotions, mood, and, ultimately, the satisfaction felt by the consumer. These three elements are also conditioned by their appropriation process and by the resulting degree of co-production and co-creation. The relative importance of each element depends on each individual. For example, studies have shown that women are more sensitive to the progressive social values conveyed by theatre or museums but place less emphasis on the elements of the service environment and that, in contrast, men give more weight to the service environment and quality (Voss and Cova, 2006). The emotions which consumers feel during the experience will give rise to satisfaction or dissatisfaction and, consequently, to the decision to repeat the experience or not. The more memorable the experience, the greater the intention to live it again.

We conclude this section with some observations on the sequence of effects which emotions produce during art consumption. The value one assigns to any given theatre or museum may depend on the emotions felt during the visit or performance. A chain of positive emotions should increase the value accorded to the product or to the cultural venue and generate an expectation of pleasure from future attendance (Bourgeon-Renault et al., 2006). As this appreciation increases, confidence in the cultural organization grows. This trust is likely to create a sense of belonging to the organization, a feeling which may eventually lead the consumer to increase their involvement gradually—by becoming a subscriber or donor, for example, or by acting as an informal spokesperson for the orchestra, theatre, or museum. A person who is heavily involved in a cultural organization will not only become a voice for it but also stand as a defender when it is criticized, undermined, or attacked. In conclusion, the act of consuming arts and culture provokes multiple emotions, and these emotions exert significant types of influence on the behaviour of consumers and on the relationships they develop with arts and culture organizations.

IMPLICATIONS FOR THE MARKETING OF ARTS AND CULTURE

The implications for the marketing of arts and culture are both simple and complex. It seems clear from the previous discussion that the role of marketing managers is to ensure the experience of the spectator or visitor is positive in terms of both the emotions generated and the positive mood stimulated by this experience. The work of art on display constitutes the basis and the central element around which the whole operation is structured; the marketing manager has no role to play. On the other hand, it is their responsibility to understand and manage all the other experiential components surrounding the show or visit. The aim is to ensure no element on the periphery of the work undermines the relationship between the person and the organization's *raison d'être*, which is the art itself. Therefore, it is necessary to control three components of good customer service: (1) physical comfort: seats, temperature, exterior noise, cleanliness of washrooms, and fluidity of operations; (2) ease of access and circulation: parking, entrances and exits, signage, coat rooms; and (3) personal relations of employees and the organization with visitors or spectators: courtesy of staff, efficient and courteous problem-solving, open and relevant channels of communication with customers.

Superior customer service ensures the artist or artwork will be approached by spectators or visitors in a good mood. In parallel, the marketing approach will foster a warm relationship with the public so the latter senses an emotional attachment to the organization and may feel "like part of the family"—to the point where they easily tolerate a show or exhibition they like less because the total experience will have presented enough interesting elements to provoke the desire to renew that experience. This tolerance for disappointment will promote customer loyalty (Obaidalahe et al., 2017).

IMPLICATIONS FOR RESEARCH

The literature on consumer experience in arts and culture appears to be oriented more towards the study of affective states (emotions, mood) than towards the study of attitudes. This is understandable to the extent that, as we have seen, artistic and cultural products are generally conceived and organized to arouse all types of emotions. But does this mean the analytical perspective of attitudinal formation put forward by Fishbein (1963) is not relevant to research in this field? We believe the answer is no. If affective states fully deserve study for the role they play in the experience of artistic and cultural consumption, then the same holds true for consumer attitudes in arts and culture. The objects that populate the field of study in arts and culture are multiple and varied, and many of them are perceived by consumers without necessarily involving an emotional response. For example, buying a ticket to see a show, examining the brochure for a concert you might attend, getting a museum membership, or planning a cultural trip abroad are all activities whose evaluation is largely based on beliefs and for which Fishbein's multi-attribute model (1963) offers a valid theoretical platform.

Curiously, the reasoned action approach (RAA) developed by Fishbein and Ajzen (2010), which aims to predict behavioural intentions on the basis of attitudes, social pressures, and individual abilities, has not had as much influence on research into arts and culture consumption as it has had on marketing and the social sciences. To be convinced, one need only consult the many meta-analyses performed by researchers in the hundreds of studies employing the theory of reasoned action (TRA; Fishbein and Ajzen, 1975) or a variant such as the RAA (Fishbein and Ajzen, 2010); the field of arts and culture has virtually no representation there. And yet this model appears to be highly relevant in many artistic and cultural contexts (e.g., Choo et al., 2016; d'Astous et al., 2005; Miesen, 2003). Indeed, from the moment the variable being explained or predicted is behavioural—an intention, for example—the TRA is relevant. It is all the more worthwhile for researchers in the field of arts and culture since the appropriate measuring instruments are readily available and easily adapted (see the appendix to the book by Fishbein and Ajzen, 2010).

To our knowledge, apart from the study by Troilo et al. (2014), the emotion typology of Richins (1997) has not been used by researchers in the marketing of arts and culture. The results of this study revealed that the emotions experienced during a theatrical performance do not generally have a direct impact on theatre attendance. While interesting, the study by Troilo et al. was limited to a subset of the Richins typology, one consisting entirely of positive emotions (e.g., joy, optimism, excitement), and to a sample of women only. In addition, it focused on a single artistic product (theatre) and examined a single dependent variable (the number of times the person visited a theatre in the last year). It therefore appears necessary to conduct new studies enabling us to learn more about the links uniting the emotions and reactions of cultural consumers. These studies should include positive and negative emotions (e.g., Richins, 1997), address a variety of artistic and cultural fields (cinema, classical music concerts, museum visits, reading, etc.), consider not only the product but the elements surrounding it as well (e.g., venue, employees), and, where possible, involve samples of participants characterized by a certain degree of heterogeneity (e.g., gender, age, and education). A particularly relevant research question here concerns how the emotions felt during the cultural consumption experience can affect the organization's brand image. For example, does the act of responding emotionally to an art exhibit have an effect on the attitude of consumers towards the organization hosting this event? As we have seen, affective states like mood operate as concepts in the associative memory network of a consumer (Bower, 1981). Therefore, following the logic of spreading activation (see Chapter 4), it is likely that the negative or positive feelings stimulated by a cultural consumption experience are propagated through the network to ultimately affect the other concepts which form it (e.g., the artist, the gallery).

Although several studies of consumer behaviour have examined the effects of mood on consumption (see Cohen et al.,

2008, for a summary), research in arts and culture seems to have neglected this variable. Yet artistic and cultural contexts are conducive to awakening this low-intensity and relatively enduring affective state. The emotions a person feels during an artistic consumption experience (e.g., at the cinema) can leave affective traces which influence their mood (Bagozzi et al., 1999). It is also possible that elements on the periphery of the artistic experience, such as music, decor, reception staff, and other participants, will stimulate a positive or negative mood. Several studies have shown that positive mood increases open-mindedness and leads to a greater propensity to take risks and seek variety (e.g., Kahn and Isen, 1993). In the context of arts and culture, this should take the form of, for example, a greater receptivity to works of art which are conceptually challenging or difficult to understand. It will be a worthwhile avenue of research to conduct studies verifying whether this is true and seeking to fully understand the role played by mood in the artistic and cultural consumer experience.

REFERENCES

Bagozzi, R. P., M. Gopinath, and P. U. Nyer (1999), "The Role of Emotions in Marketing", *Journal of the Academy of Marketing Science*, 27 (2), 184–206.

Baker, J. (1986), "The Role of the Environment in Marketing Services: The Consumer Perspective", in J. A. Czepiel, C. A. Congram, and J. Shanahan (eds.), *The Services Challenge: Integrating for Competitive Advantage*, Chicago, IL: American Marketing Association, pp. 79–84.

Bourgeon-Renault, D., C. Urbain, C. Petr, M. Le Gall-Ely, and A. Gombault (2006), "An Experiential Approach to the Consumption Value of Arts and Culture: The Case of Museums and Monuments", *International Journal of Arts Management*, 9 (1), 35–47.

Bower, G. H. (1981), "Mood and Memory", *American Psychologist*, 26, 129–148.

Chan, E. K. (2019), "The Role of Personal Relevance in the Value Creation Process of Edutainment Consumption", *Journal Consumer Behavior*, 18 (3), 190–204.

Choo, H., K. Ahn, and J. F. Petrick (2016), "An Integrated Model of Festival Revisit Intentions: Theory of Planned Behavior and Festival Quality/Satisfaction", *International Journal of Contemporary Hospitality Management*, 28 (4), 818–838.

Cohen, J. B., M. T. Pham, and E. d'Andrade (2008), "The Nature and Role of Affect in Consumer Behavior", in C. P. Haugtvedt, P. M. Herr, and

F. R. Kardes (eds.), *Handbook of Consumer Psychology*, New York, NY: Erlbaum, pp. 297–348.

Colbert, F. and D. C. Dantas (2019), "Customer Relationships in Arts Marketing: A Review of Key Dimensions in Delivery by Artistic and Cultural Organizations", *International Journal of Arts Management*, 21 (2), 4–14.

d'Astous, A., F. Colbert, and D. Montpetit (2005), "Music Piracy on the Web—How Effective Are Anti-Piracy Arguments? Evidence from the Theory of Planned Behavior", *Journal of Consumer Policy*, 28 (3), 289–310.

d'Astous, A., N. Daghfous, P. Balloffet, and C. Boulaire (2018), *Comportement du consommateur*, 5e édition, Montréal: Chenelière Éducation.

Debenedetti, S. (2003), "Investigating the Role of Companions in the Art Museum Experience", *International Journal of Arts Management*, 5 (3), 52–63.

Derbaix, C. (1995), "L'impact des réactions affectives induites par les messages publicitaires: Une analyse tenant compte de l'implication", *Recherche et Applications en Marketing*, 10 (2), 3–30.

Fishbein, M. (1963), "An Investigation of the Relationship between Beliefs about an Object and the Attitude toward That Object", *Human Relations*, 16, 233–240.

Fishbein, M. and I. Ajzen (1975), *Belief, Attitude, Intention, and Behavior: An Introduction to Theory and Research*, Reading, MA: Addison-Wesley.

Fishbein, M. and I. Ajzen (2010), *Predicting and Changing Behavior: The Reasoned Action Approach*, New York, NY: Psychology Press.

Gainer, B. (1995), "Rituals and Relationships: Interpersonal Influences on Shared Consumption", *Journal of Business Research*, 32 (3), 253–260.

Isen, A. M. (1984), "Toward Understanding the Role of Affect in Cognition", in R. S. Wyer, Jr. and T. K. Srull (eds.), *Handbook of Social Cognition, Volume 3*, Hillsdale, NJ: Erlbaum, pp. 179–236.

Isen, A. M. (2008), "Positive Affect and Decision Processes: Some Recent Theoretical Developments with Practical Implications", in C. P. Haugtvedt, P. M. Herr, and F. R. Kardes (2008), *Handbook of Consumer Psychology*, New York, NY: Erlbaum, pp. 273–296.

Kahn, B. and A. M. Isen (1993), "The Influence of Positive Affect on Variety-Seeking among Safe, Enjoyable Products", *Journal of Consumer Research*, 20 (2), 257–270.

Mehrabian, A. and J. A. Russell (1974), *An Approach to Environmental Psychology*, Cambridge, MA: MIT Press.

Miesen, H. W. J. M. (2003), "Predicting and Explaining Literary Reading: An Application of the Theory of Planned Behavior", *Poetics*, 31 (3–4), 189–212.

Minkiewicz, J., K. Bridson, and J. Evans (2016), "Co-Production of Service Experiences: Insights from the Cultural Sector", *Journal of Services Marketing*, 30 (7), 749–761.

Minkiewicz, J., J. Evans, and K. Bridson (2014), "How Do Consumers Co-Create Their Experiences? An Exploration in the Heritage Sector", *Journal of Marketing Management*, 30 (1–2), 30–59.

Obaidalahe, Z., F. Salerno, and F. Colbert (2017), "Subscribers' Overall Evaluation of a Multi-Experience Cultural Service, Tolerance for Disappointment and Sustainable Loyalty", *International Journal of Arts Management*, 20 (1), 21–30.

Richins, M. L. (1997), "Measuring Emotions in the Consumption Experience", *Journal of Consumer Research*, 24 (2), 127–146.

Troilo, G., M. C. Cito, and I. Soscia (2014), "Repurchase Behavior in the Performing Arts: Do Emotions Matter without Involvement?", *Psychology & Marketing*, 31 (8), 635–646.

Voss, Z. G. and V. Cova (2006), "How Sex Differences in Perceptions Influence Customer Satisfaction: A Study of Theatre Audiences", *Marketing Theory*, 6 (2), 201–21.

Wang, Y. J. and M. S. Minor (2008), "Validity, Reliability, and Applicability of Psychophysiological Techniques in Marketing Research", *Psychology & Marketing*, 25 (2), 197–232.

Zanna, M. P. and J. K. Rempel (1988), "Attitudes: A New Look at an Old Concept", in A. Bar-Tal and A. Kruglansky (eds.), *The Social Psychology of Knowledge*, Cambridge, MA: Cambridge University Press, pp. 315–334.

Decision-making

Chapter 6

This chapter examines decision-making—by consumers in general, and by arts and culture consumers in particular. First, we present a general model of the consumer decision process, to serve as a foundation for discussion of the major topics. Next, we summarize the key findings made by researchers investigating how this decision process operates in arts and culture. In the concluding sections, we discuss some practical implications for marketing in this field and suggest new avenues for theoretical research.

THE CONSUMER DECISION PROCESS

To introduce this topic, let us consider the following fictitious story.

> John and Sarah have just arrived at their hotel in the heart of Manhattan. For this young couple, a weekend in New York is a dream come true—but now the reality is upon them. They have to plan their activities, most of which are cultural (they are both dedicated fans of the visual arts). Where to begin?
>
> As far as Sarah is concerned, there's no room for debate. For years, she has dreamt of visiting New York's famous Museum of Modern Art (MoMA). John is fine with that, but says they need to consider the other options beforehand ("He always takes the analytical approach," Sarah thinks). He suggests they check the TimeOut website since it includes a rundown of the Big Apple's best museums among its listings.
>
> Sarah is forced to admit it: the information on the site is quite relevant. But with wicked glee she points at the screen and says, "Oh look, John, the MoMA is the first museum on

DOI: 10.4324/9780429263118-9

their list—how about that, eh?" After comparing three options (the MoMA, the Guggenheim Museum, and the Brooklyn Museum) under different criteria (proximity, ticket costs, current exhibitions), they choose to visit the MoMA first—which draws a wry smile from Sarah.

Later that day, back at the hotel, John and Sarah both agree they had a fantastic experience at the MoMA. Sarah has only one regret: in the museum shop, she chose to buy a souvenir tote bag rather than a reproduction of a work by Miró, an artist she particularly admires. This reproduction was beautiful, she says, but too expensive—and anyway, the tote bag is really cool.

This narrative describes a typical situation where consumers are making decisions. It aims to exemplify, among other things, the fact that many consumer decisions are characterized by stages which follow a sequential pattern. The model shown in Figure 6.1 summarizes these stages; it will serve as the foundation for our discussion in this section of the chapter.

Recognizing a need

The decision process is initiated when the consumer has a need to fulfil. We use the term "need", though in many situations it is actually a desire which is involved, not a need. For example, John and Sarah want to visit museums; one might argue they do not really need to. What is important to note, however, is their awareness at this stage that the current state of things (*we are at the hotel*) is different from the desired state (*we want to visit a museum*) and that, to close this gap, they must take action.

Figure 6.1 A model of the consumer decision process.

The stage of recognizing a need is necessarily something personal; it depends on the person and the situation they find themselves in. It is also a stage with different degrees of urgency. For example, John and Sarah have only a weekend to spend in New York City; hence, their need to identify which museum to visit is pressing and quite urgent. For other people in a similar situation, this decision might be less urgent.

Searching for information

The model shown in Figure 6.1 postulates the search for information as the next step in the consumer decision process. When this search draws from information in one's memory, it is called *internal search*. For example, Sarah does not have to search very long, because in her long-term memory she has already categorized the MoMA as the museum to see. John, however, suggests collecting information from an external source, in this case from a website. They could also have consulted other sources of external information such as brochures, newspapers, or the concierge at their hotel.

The many studies addressing information search in consumer decision-making have largely focused on this external type (for a summary, see Solomon, 2017). Their results suggest that the intensity of the search (a variable measured by the number of sources consulted) depends on several factors, including the time available, the ease of finding information, the importance of the decision, and consumers' past experience of searching externally. Some people have a personality which makes them more likely to search than others (e.g., John is a very analytical person, according to Sarah). In general, scholars believe the degree of external search rests on a comparative analysis of the costs and benefits associated with this activity. Thus, the greater the benefits of searching relative to the costs involved (time, money, mental work, physical effort, etc.), the more intense the search will be.

Table 6.1 Position of three museums in relation to three selection criteria

	Evaluation of alternatives		
Selection criteria	MoMA	Guggenheim	Brooklyn
Proximity	1.3 km	4.2 km	8.0 km
Cost of tickets	C$100	C$100	C$45
Exhibitions	3	1	1

Consumers may seek any kind of information, but researchers generally agree on two main types: the identification of alternatives (for John and Sarah, it was the MoMA, the Guggenheim Museum, and the Brooklyn Museum), and the selection of criteria (in their case, it was proximity, cost of tickets, and current exhibitions). Research studies on the subject often present this information in a matrix format, as shown in Table 6.1.

Analysis and decision

We know that John and Sarah eventually opted for a visit to the MoMA, but the story does not tell us how they arrived at their choice. It is likely they combined the information collected from the TimeOut site (see Table 6.1) so as to determine what option would appear best. Marketing researchers believe consumers use mental procedures in their decision-making—called *decision rules*—in a more or less systematic manner so they can discern the different alternatives available to them. For example, perhaps John and Sarah chose to visit the MoMA because proximity, for them, was the most important criterion and this museum was the best option in that regard. If so, they were using what is called the *lexicographic rule*, meaning they ranked the decision criteria in order of importance and then chose the best alternative from those qualifying on the top-ranking criterion. Other types of decision rules are possible (Solomon, 2017), and their application may lead to different choices. Consumers sometimes use shortcuts to simplify their lives. For example, were John and Sarah influenced by the fact that the MoMA was the first museum on the TimeOut list? These rules of simplification, called *heuristics*, are useful—for example, when time is short or you do not feel like racking your brain—but they can give rise to choices which are less than optimal (see Gilovich et al., 2002).

Consumption and post-decision processes

Consumption is a concept which has a number of different meanings. It may refer to a purchase, to a lived experience (as John and Sarah had), or to the use of a product. Regardless of how consumption takes place, it is likely to give rise to reflections and questions. Did I make the right choice? Will I buy this brand again in the future? Will I recommend this museum to my friends?

Two post-decision processes have been of particular interest to researchers in consumer behaviour: satisfaction and cognitive dissonance. The first is a subjective evaluation of the consumption experience. When this evaluation is positive, it means the consumer is satisfied. When it is negative, they are dissatisfied. Many researchers believe satisfaction is a state of mind resulting from a comparison between what the consumer expected and what they received (Johnson, 1998). Thus, fulfilled or surpassed expectations (e.g., *this museum is much more interesting than I thought it would be*) lead to a feeling of satisfaction, while unfulfilled expectations produce dissatisfaction. Satisfaction and dissatisfaction also significantly affect how consumers will behave towards a brand in the future, mainly with regard to repurchase intention, loyalty (see Chapter 4), potential complaints, and recommendations to other people. For this reason, most companies strive to measure customer satisfaction regularly and make changes to their offer in order to maintain an acceptable level of satisfaction.

Consumers sometimes have doubts about the decision they have made. Sarah, for example, wonders whether she ought to have bought the reproduction of Miró's painting rather than the souvenir tote bag. This type of post-decision evaluation creates a feeling of discomfort caused by *cognitive dissonance*, a situation where a person must adjust to conflicting attitudes, beliefs, or behaviours (Cooper, 2007). Thus, for Sarah, her purchase of the tote bag is in conflict with her belief that the reproduction was a better option. The discomfort resulting from cognitive dissonance will be greater if the decision is irrevocable, difficult, or important. The greater the discomfort, the more motivated the consumer will be to reduce the dissonance. To do so, they can adopt a variety of mental strategies, such as diminishing the importance of the decision, increasing the perceived value of the chosen option (note how Sarah says the bag is cool), or decreasing the perceived value of the other options (she tells herself the reproduction was too expensive).

Some remarks about the consumer decision process

The model shown in Figure 6.1 is a useful but greatly simplified representation of the events which occur during the consumer decision process. First, it should be noted that the perspective adopted by this model is essentially individual. But in many situations where consumer decisions need to be made, more than one person participates. The model can partly accommodate multiple actors, as our analysis of the made-up narrative featuring John and Sarah shows, but let us bear in mind that certain elements inherent in group decision-making, such as conflict, compromise, and task-sharing, are not explicitly considered there.

It must also be recognized that not all decisions require consumers to pass through all the stages of the decision process shown in Figure 6.1. The complexity of the process will vary depending on the consumer's experience. Thus, we can distinguish three types of decision: habitual (the process is a routine followed many times in the past); moderately difficult (the product category is known, but an information search for options and selection criteria is required); and complex (little is known about the product category, options, and criteria). This typology, adapted from the work of John Howard (Howard and Sheth, 1969), helps us understand why a decision which is complex for some people will appear very simple for others.

A third limitation of the model in Figure 6.1 is its focus—it only considers a single decision. However, it often happens that several decisions must be made at almost the same time. In addition, a decision taken regarding a given object may provoke the need to make other decisions. For example, what mode of transportation shall we choose for travelling to the museum? How shall we buy the tickets? What current exhibitions will we see? Where will we eat? What souvenirs will we buy? Although the model shown can accommodate various situations where multiple decisions need to be made, it does not explicitly take this into account.

A final remark about the model concerns its rationalist character. Many researchers in consumer behaviour believe this representation is very limiting because it ignores the playful, aesthetic, exploratory, emotional, and imaginative dimensions which are generally associated with consumption (Holbrook and Hirschman, 1982). This model depicts a rational consumer collecting and analysing data, and employing mental rules to achieve an optimal choice; it does not depict a human being motivated by pleasure-seeking and by the need to socialize, make discoveries, and feel emotion. We agree in part with this criticism, but we also consider it less significant than some scholars believe. As we saw in Chapter 1, the consumption of artistic or cultural products can be approached by examining three groups of variables: the social environment, the psyche, and the experience. In this last group, we include affect, learning, and decision-making. The experiential aspects of consumption (Holbrook and Hirschman, 1982) can also, in our view, be discerned within these three fundamental processes. Although the decision process model we present in this chapter does not focus directly on the experiential aspects of consumption, this does not mean it excludes these aspects from the activities which encompass consumer decision-making.

DECISION-MAKING IN THE FIELD OF ARTS AND CULTURE

Consumers interested in a play, concert, or film are faced with the fact that what companies present is always geared towards the new. The essential motivation for the artists also comes from a desire to surpass what others have done, offer a new reading of a work, or convey a different perspective. In deciding whether to buy a ticket or not, or what to choose from all the available alternatives, consumers with an interest in arts and culture have only a little information to work with. They cannot test the new artistic product as they would test a regular consumer good. They can view or listen to excerpts from films, plays, or concerts, but these excerpts are usually cherry-picked and edited to whet the appetite of potential viewers—a strategy whose effectiveness, incidentally, has not been demonstrated (Euzéby and Martinez, 2004).

In the example of John and Sarah, the couple must choose among several museum venues. In addition to weighing their interest in the exhibits, John and Sarah consider variables such as the entrance fee, the distance to the chosen venue, and the time available to them. There is great pressure upon them to make the right choice. While logistical questions are relatively easy to answer, the aesthetic choice among several different exhibits is less so.

The challenge for cultural consumers thus becomes how to make an informed choice. When a new play, film, or concert is announced, consumers can find relevant information in three ways: using their prior knowledge of the art form, consulting reviews and other documentation, or relying on word-of-mouth.

Some consumers will have a very good knowledge of the art form, which allows them to make a decision based on factual elements accumulated over the course of their frequent attendance. They may know this choreographer's approach, have already attended a concert of this symphonic work, be a fan of this actor, or be unconditional fans of opera. However, a great many consumers do not have the tools to make informed decisions. Cultural organizations rely heavily on critical reviews to inform consumers who are less equipped to judge on their own. Critics are also thought to have an important influence on ticket sales, no doubt because there is a strong belief that an expert's opinion can play an important role in the success or failure of a show. In fact, while many consumers rely on critical reviews when making their choice, not all of them do. The critic's role has more nuance than may first be apparent (d'Astous, 1999; d'Astous and Colbert, 2002; d'Astous et al., 2007). Consumers with a large reservoir of knowledge will often consult the reviews *after* attending the show. This sequence allows them to compare their own independent evaluation with that of professionals. Other consumers who are less expert or more cautious will read several reviews and then decide to rely on them if the critics present a consensus of opinion. If they find no consensus, these consumers will either risk buying a ticket anyway or find someone they know who can inform them. Others will do both, and consult the critical reviews while also seeking opinions from people they trust. Still others will rely only on the opinion of the people they know.

In general, consumers who consult a critical review go beyond the evaluation it provides; they seek to understand the reasons why the critic has taken a particular position (d'Astous and Touil,

1999). Thus, when a critic who is usually mild or positive in their judgement suddenly writes a negative review, it will have a greater impact on the purchase intentions of the readers. On the other hand, if the critic makes only positive comments about a show, in their habitual way, the review is not likely to have any influence on the reader at all.

From a psychological point of view, the impact of criticism on the future spectator depends on their confidence in their own judgement and on their sensitivity to the views of others. People who trust their own opinion because they believe they have sufficient knowledge will likely be impervious to the views of the critic. Those who have less confidence in their ability to properly evaluate an artistic offer may want to reassure themselves by seeking information from critics or peers.

In addition to the degree of self-confidence, people who are sensitive to social influence are more influenced by critics (d'Astous and Colbert, 2002). This sensitivity to critics affects two aspects: the acquisition of relevant information (informational social influence) and the desire to comply with social norms (normative social influence; Deutsch and Gerard, 1955). The more the consumer believes that others can provide useful information, the greater their tendency to consult with critics and peers. Likewise, the more social pressure consumers feel from others, the more they will seek to reinforce their views by consulting the critics or by seeking the opinions of people who, they are convinced, have the same tastes as they do. Many consumer decisions are influenced by the views of other people when the latter are perceived to be capable of providing relevant information on products or services (Bearden and Etzel, 1982). This opinion will be solicited and valued more when the consumer has less confidence in their own judgement and greater trust in that of the person whom they consult. By taking the views of others into account, the consumer accumulates useful information while maintaining or strengthening social ties. This sensitivity to other people can also influence the choice of one theatre from among a group of theatres; some consumers are looking for venues where they will find people similar to themselves (Gainer, 1995). While the theatre season and its productions have their significance, the possibility of socializing with people similar to us seems to figure among the criteria considered in the decision process of cultural consumers.

Expert opinions and word-of-mouth

With regard to critics, it is interesting to note that the opinions of experts are comparable to those of ordinary spectators, as several studies have shown. Research conducted with opera fans have revealed that the evaluations of fans and experts are essentially similar, the difference being mainly in the ability of experts to take more aspects of opera production into account than fans can do (Boerner and Renz, 2008). Another research study has shown that in the case of films, the evaluations made by small groups of fans correlate more closely with the success of a film than do the evaluations produced by small groups of experts (Escoffier and McKelvey, 2015).

One question which often arises for an organization, when critics deliver negative reviews, concerns the best attitude to adopt in response. The results of one study on this issue suggest that organizations should not hide negative reviews but be transparent with their audience. While consumers respond favourably to the disclosure of negative criticism, they evaluate negatively the strategy of only publishing excerpts from positive criticism and not mentioning negative criticism. It appears this latter approach may diminish trust in the organization, whereas negative criticism would be perceived neither positively nor negatively (Wiggins et al., 2017).

Word-of-mouth, as the presence of social media grows more pervasively, is becoming a powerful factor influencing the consumer decision process. The speaker or poster may base their message on functional aspects (such as ease of access or availability of washrooms), price, emotion, social environment, or novelty of the product. However, the consumer who receives the message needs to have confidence in its source. The more the Internet user identifies themselves with the group that takes a position on the Internet, the greater the influence of this group will be. This effect, whether positive or negative, is also more significant when the affective value of the experience is stronger than its cognitive value. Word-of-mouth is most powerful when it conveys emotional values generated by the co-creation of experience. It then becomes part of this co-creation process (Rajaobelina et al., 2019).

Consumer satisfaction in the field of arts and culture

As we saw in the previous chapter, the satisfaction of the patron comes mainly from the positive emotions they feel while attending a show or visiting an exhibition. It is the work of art itself, above all, which produces this emotion. And yet, since the act of attending a theatre or museum is usually not performed alone, sharing the experience with a loved one or with friends also contributes to satisfaction. Similarly, the physical environment and the quality of customer service are important contributors (Hume, 2008). Satisfaction is therefore a multidimensional response to the work, the environment, and the social experience, and these elements form the whole which we call the overall experience of the spectator or the visitor (Colbert and Dantas, 2019; Obaidalahe et al., 2017).

To balance this conception of the drivers of satisfaction, we must add other behaviours tied to the motivations which inspire a consumer to buy a ticket. Thus, while dedicated classical music fans may be loyal to a particular orchestra without much regard for other elements, people seeking a leisure experience alone will probably pay more attention to the quality of customer service.

Consumer loyalty in the field of arts and culture

Loyalty means returning to the same theatre or to the same museum (e.g., by becoming a subscribing member), but it can also be understood as loyalty to a form of art. Thus, the relational customer will want to establish a relationship with a company because they find satisfaction in a predictable seasonal programme and in feeling they are part of a community which resembles them. On the other hand, the transactional customer will be loyal to a form of art, but not necessarily to a particular company or museum. Unlike the former, the latter does not look for satisfaction in what is predictable. They are looking for novelty, for works of art that challenge their feelings and intellect. Loyalty to a particular institution will not be of interest to them. The relational customer, on the contrary, will want to establish this relationship, which is why the quality of customer service matters to them very much, unlike the transactional spectator (Voss et al, 2006).

IMPLICATIONS FOR THE MARKETING OF ARTS AND CULTURE

We have seen, in this chapter, that a variety of elements influence the consumer decision process. Given these elements, and what we have learned from the start of the book, we can examine this process by means of a hierarchical representation or tree diagram (Figure 6.2).

We mentioned earlier that consumer decisions are likely to vary in their level of difficulty. The buyer behaviour typology formulated by Howard and Sheth (1969) distinguishes between habitual decision-making, limited problem-solving, and extensive problem-solving. In general, it is recognized that consumers will be more involved in the decision process when the complexity of the task is great or the issue is important. For example, deciding to spend an evening at the theatre commits the consumer to a certain level of involvement, much more than buying an inexpensive commodity which does not require a strong emotional investment. For this reason, two levels of involvement (high and low) are distinguished in the model shown in Figure 6.2. When the consumer's involvement is low, the decision process will either be automatic (habitual) or we can say this will merely be an incidental

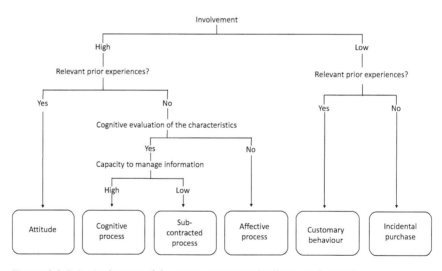

Figure 6.2 Principal types of decision processes (Colbert et al., 1993).

Source: Colbert et al. (2007), *Marketing Culture and the Arts*, 3rd Edition, Carmelle and Rémi-Marcoux Chair in Arts Management, HEC Montréal, Montréal, Canada.

purchase. In some situations, such as a trip to a performing arts venue or museum, the involvement will be stronger because the risk is greater. Two categories of spectators or visitors can be defined: consumers who have relevant previous experience and those who do not. Opera aficionados or the fans of a pop music idol will not need much encouragement when deciding to buy a ticket. Since these consumers have already developed a strong positive attitude towards their favourite opera or their pop idol, they will quickly purchase tickets once promoters announce a new show. Consumers who have not developed this strong attitude can be divided into three groups. First, there are those who have the ability to judge the offer because they have sufficient points of reference or experience in relation to the art form or the organization in question. They will then make use of factual elements (director, conductor, playwright, visual artist, etc.) to make their decision. In the model shown in Figure 6.2, this is called the cognitive process. Those consumers who have a limited ability to search for and understand the information necessary for decision-making are likely to use a subordinate mode. For example, they will consult their friends, read the critical reviews, or do both. These people rely on the judgement of others in their decision-making (subcontracted process). Finally, there are the consumers who do not proceed like these previous groups—they make their decisions based on what looks interesting. This affective process is active when, for example, a person watches a media advertisement or a film trailer and says, "This exhibition (or this film) looks good, I would like to go and see it". Another example could be a stage play which becomes very popular, such that when additional performances are announced, it leads potential consumers to conclude that the play must be good to have earned these extra shows.

The six groups defined in the model shown in Figure 6.2 correspond to six different market segments. With regard to the group of consumers who have a strong positive attitude towards the product, we simply need to inform them; we do not need to persuade them. For consumers who use cognitive processes, marketers must provide the factual information they will use as the basis for making their decision. For those who use the opinions of their friends and acquaintances, or rely on the work of critics, marketers will need to highlight the favourable reviews and find a way to generate word-of-mouth. For consumers who depend on the affective process (those in the fourth market segment), it is appropriate to use arguments that stimulate an affective response (e.g., *the show everyone is raving about* or *the hit film of the summer*). As for the last two situations, one might think they do not really apply to the cultural sector. Going to the theatre is not an everyday consumer activity, and cultural consumption rarely qualifies as an incidental purchase, even though one can imagine situations where we happen to visit the museum gift shop and decide on a whim to buy a souvenir, or times when we are browsing in a bookstore and a new title catches our eye.

IMPLICATIONS FOR RESEARCH

The decision process model presented in this chapter (Figure 6.1) suggests several research questions which merit future study. Do we know how dedicated cultural consumers (e.g., opera aficionados) initiate the need recognition stage of their decision process? Does it depend on the type of product they are contemplating? Can we apply the typology of John Howard to marketing the arts and culture? How can organizations in this field benefit more from the results of such research?

In situations where consumers make decisions regarding artistic and cultural products, the information search stage is crucial. How do consumers obtain the information they need for making an informed decision? To what extent and how intensely do they seek information? What kind of information do they seek? What are the characteristics of consumers who search extensively for external information? How do they obtain this external information? Does it depend on the type of products they are contemplating? How can cultural organizations benefit from the answers to these research questions?

Studies are also needed to understand how cultural consumers analyse and combine the information they obtain so they can make the best choices. Are the decision rules which have been identified in the consumer behaviour literature appropriate for describing the behaviour of dedicated cultural consumers? What factors explain why consumers choose to follow one decision rule and not another? How can arts and culture organizations benefit from this knowledge?

Finally, there is a need for research investigating what happens after cultural products have been consumed. How do consumers build their post-purchase impressions? What is the impact of satisfaction levels on future purchases and the organization's brand image? Is the concept of cognitive dissonance relevant to the field of arts and culture? If so, in what situations is it relevant? How do consumers manage their level of cognitive dissonance? How can cultural organizations make sure their customers are satisfied?

REFERENCES

Bearden, W. O. and M. J. Etzel (1982), "Reference Group Influence on Product and Brand Purchase Decisions", *Journal of Consumer Research*, 9 (2), 183–194.

Boerner, S. and S. Renz (2008), "Performance Measurement in Opera Companies: Comparing the Subjective Quality Judgements of Experts and Non-experts", *International Journal of Arts Management*, 10 (3), 21–37.

Colbert, F. and D. C. Dantas (2019), "Customer Relationships in Arts Marketing: A Review of Key Dimensions in Delivery by Artistic and Cultural Organizations", *International Journal of Arts Management*, 21 (2), 4–14.

Colbert, F. et al. (1993), *Marketing Culture and the Arts*, 1st edition, Montreal: Carmelle and Rémi-Marcoux Chair in Arts Management, HEC Montréal.

Cooper, J. (2007), *Cognitive Dissonance: Fifty Years of a Classic Theory*, Los Angeles, CA: Sage.

d'Astous, A. (1999), "A Study of Individual Factors Explaining Movie Goers' Consultation of Film Critics", in B. Dubois, T. M. Lowrey, L. J. Shrum, and M. Vanhuele (eds.), *European Advances in Consumer Research Volume 4*, Provo, UT: Association for Consumer Research, pp. 201–207.

d'Astous, A. and F. Colbert (2002), "Moviegoers' Consultation of Critical Reviews: Psychological Antecedents and Consequences", *International Journal of Arts Management*, 5 (1), 24–35.

d'Astous, A., F. Colbert, and V. Nobert (2007), "Country-Movie Genre Congruence Effects on the Evaluation of Upcoming Movies: The Moderating Role of Critical Reviews and Moviegoers' Prior Knowledge", *International Journal of Arts Management*, 10 (1), 45–51.

d'Astous, A. and N. Touil (1999), "Consumer Evaluations of Movies on the Basis of Critics' Judgments", *Psychology & Marketing*, 16 (8), 677–694.

Deutsch, M. and H. B. Gerard (1955), "A Study of Normative and Informational Social Influences upon Individual Judgment", *Journal of Abnormal and Social Psychology*, 51 (3), 629–636.

Escoffier, N. and B. McKelvey (2015), "The Wisdom of Crowds in the Movie Industry: Towards New Solutions to Reduce Uncertainties", *International Journal of Arts Management*, 17 (2), 52–63.

Euzéby, F. and C. Martinez (2004), "La bande-annonce cinématographique: Quel impact sur la décision d'aller voir le film? Une étude exploratoire", *Décisions Marketing*, 33, 39–50.

Gainer, B. (1995), "Rituals and Relationships: Interpersonal Influences on Shared Consumption", *Journal of Business Research*, 32 (3), 253–260.

Gilovich, T., D. Griffin, and D. Kahneman (eds.) (2002), *Heuristics and Biases: The Psychology of Intuitive Judgment*, New York, NY: Cambridge University Press.

Holbrook, M. B. and E. C. Hirschman (1982), "The Experiential Aspects of Consumption: Consumer Fantasies, Feelings and Fun", *Journal of Consumer Research*, 9 (2), 132–140.

Howard, J. A. and J. N. Sheth (1969), *The Theory of Buyer Behavior*, New York, NY: John Wiley & Sons.

Hume, M. (2008), "Developing a Conceptual Model for Repurchase Intention in the Performing Arts: The Roles of Emotion, Core Service and Service Delivery", *International Journal of Arts Management*, 10 (2), 40–55.

Johnson, M. D. (1998), *Customer Orientation and Market Action*, Upper Saddle River, NJ: Prentice-Hall.

Obaidalahe, Z., F. Salerno, and F. Colbert (2017), "Subscribers' Overall Evaluation of a Multi-Experience Cultural Service, Tolerance for Disappointment and Sustainable Loyalty", *International Journal of Arts Management*, 20 (1), 21–30.

Rajaobelina, L., P. Dusseault, and L. Ricard (2019), "The Mediating Role of Place Attachment in Experience and Word of Mouth: The Case of Music and Film Festivals", *International Journal of Arts Management*, 21 (2), 43–54.

Solomon, M. R. (2017), *Consumer Behavior: Buying, Having, and Being*, 12th edition, Upper Saddle River, NJ: Pearson Education.

Voss, G. B., M. Montoya-Weiss, and Z. G. Voss (2006), "Aligning Innovation with Market Characteristics in the Nonprofit Professional Theater Industry", *Journal of Marketing Research*, 43, 296–302.

Wiggins, J., C. Song, D. Trivedi, and S. B. Preece (2017), "Consumer Perceptions of Arts Organizations' Strategies for Responding to Online Reviews", *International Journal of Arts Management*, 20 (1), 4–20.

THE SOCIAL ENVIRONMENT

Part 4

Reference groups, culture, and subcultures
Chapter 7

In this chapter, we discuss a major topic of research into the behaviour of cultural consumers: the direct or indirect influences of the social environment. First, we will discuss this topic in a general way by examining the influences which originate from the people around us: family, colleagues, friends, and other members of our habitual or situational social environment. We shall do so by employing the concept of *reference groups*. Next, we shall look at the ubiquitous but generally less obvious influence of *culture* and *subcultures*. Last, we shall look at how marketing researchers have applied these concepts to the study of arts consumption and at the lessons that can be drawn from their results for practical applications and new research.

REFERENCE GROUPS

Since the beginnings of social psychology as a formal discipline, researchers have been drawn to the question of how other people influence and affect our individual behaviour. A major figure in this field is the American psychologist Solomon Asch. In the 1950s, he conducted a series of original studies designed to illuminate the processes which lead a person to adopt the beliefs, preferences, and behaviours of other people in their social environment (Asch, 1955).

DOI: 10.4324/9780429263118-11

In one typical study, a person is taking part in a psychological research experiment she believes to involve perceptual tasks based on her visual judgement. She is seated around a table with six other participants. Facing them is the experimenter, who asks them to identify which of three straight vertical lines appearing on a board is closer in length to a fourth line shown to the side—a task of absurd simplicity. The woman is unaware that all the other participants are confederates working secretly with the experimenter. One by one, they tell the experimenter—in a loud voice and without hesitation—that one particular line (they all pick the same one) is equal in length to the fourth line, even though objectively it is not. As the only real subject of this experiment, she has been carefully positioned so that she must be the last to express herself.

The purpose of the study was to see whether the pressure exerted by a group of strangers during social interaction can cause someone to alter their judgement and conform to that of the group, despite objective evidence that the altered judgement is wrong. In the studies conducted by Solomon Asch, about 40% of the people conformed to the majority. In the control groups, which contained only one participant at a time and no confederates playing a role, there was virtually no error in the perceptual task.

It is useful to contrast this social conformity research with a study carried out several years later by Venkatesan (1966) in a marketing context. The experimental procedure was similar to the one employed by Asch, except that commercial products were used as the critical stimuli. Specifically, participants were shown three completely identical business suits and asked to choose the best one. Participants were informed that the suits were manufactured by different companies, that real differences in quality were present, and that studies had shown experienced consumers could identify the best of the three. About 50% of the "real" participants in this study complied with the group's opinion.

When we look closely, we see there is a significant difference between this study and the experiments conducted by Asch. The older studies employed critical stimuli with easily spotted objective differences, whereas in the Venkatesan study (1966) there were no objective differences between the suits.

Furthermore, the influence processes elicited in these experiments are different. In Asch's studies, the group exerts pressure for the person to align his or her judgement with that of the group—a modification representing true behavioural compliance. In contrast, in the Venkatesan study (1966), the group serves as a source of information and the behaviour is more like a form of acceptance or internalization. In both cases, the group acts as a reference which the person uses like scaffolding to construct their judgement.

This long introduction has, we hope, enabled us to show that the influence of other people on our behaviour can manifest itself in diverse ways. We will discuss this topic later in this chapter. For the moment, let us examine the concept of a reference group on the basis of the following definition: individuals or groups with whom a consumer self-compares to better define his or her own beliefs, values, attitudes, and behaviours.

First, it should be emphasized that, as the term "reference group" indicates, the main characteristic here is that of a comparison. Not every group can be described as a reference group; it must be a group which someone employs for purposes of comparison with their own behaviour. Thus, one particular group will act as a reference for one person but not for another.

In previous chapters on consumer attitudes and decision-making, we have placed great emphasis on the role of information. We have seen, for example, that consumer attitudes are formed from their beliefs and those beliefs are based on information. Similarly, we have seen that consumers make decisions by considering the information they have about the selection criteria as well as how different options are positioned on these criteria. It is important, however, to realize that this information, which is so crucial to the functioning of consumers, is *filtered* through the social environment. The signals we gather from the world around us are often unclear or ambiguous, so we call upon other people to help us interpret that information. The resulting perceptions thus become socially validated. People do not like uncertainty—they want to maintain unequivocal behavioural orientations towards their acts (Jones and Gerard, 1967), and reference groups allow them to achieve this goal.

Consider the example of a man who loves fine arts but discovers, during a visit to a museum, an abstract painting which he finds difficult to understand. He does not know whether he likes this painting or not. He may find it pretty or he may find it ugly. But ugliness, like beauty, is a relative quality; it is defined essentially through "the eye of the beholders". It varies according to cultures, fashions, and eras. A reference group—in our current example, it could be a well-informed museum guide—can remove or at least mitigate the ambiguity associated with artistic appreciation and many other activities.

Although the definition of reference group suggests it must be a *physical* entity, this is not a necessary condition. A reference group can be abstract to some degree (e.g., academic writers, tourists, art collectors, artists) and even imaginary. But when the reference group corresponds to a real physical entity (such as one's colleagues at work), it is usually the mental representation that counts.

We can draw a parallel here with the self-concept we discussed in Chapter 2. The self-concept involves a kind of schema or mental representation of oneself. This representative image can be descriptive or idealized. An actual person may be attached to the self-concept, but this is secondary—it is the mental image that counts. The same principle applies to reference groups.

There are different types:

- Aspirational groups, which contain people you would like to resemble (e.g., art fans, cinephiles, music lovers).
- Membership groups, which contain the people in your social network (e.g., the circles of friends and family to which you belong).
- Dissociative groups: These are groups which you do not identify with or which you expressly dislike being associated with (e.g., snobs, fans of kitsch art, tacky dressers).

It is important to realize that the status of a reference group can change, depending on the situation. Reference groups are not fixed; like the apostle Peter, who three times denied knowing Christ when questioned by Roman soldiers, a person can disavow a group in a given situation. For example, suppose that in a chic New York art gallery, a fashion-conscious art connoisseur sees "specimens" of his membership group (some fellow fans of the fine art scene) arrive wearing Bermuda shorts and loud floral print shirts. Suddenly, and in this particular situation, he may want to dissociate himself from this group.

Consumption plays an important role in how a group is defined and how a person relates with a group. For example, teenagers will choose the clothes they wear not only for their functional utility but also for what these clothes say about their relationship with one or more reference groups. A teenager who wears a particular brand of shoes may be signalling to others that she belongs to a group, share the values of that group, or aspires to belong to it.

Consumer objects and consumption itself play an important role in how reference groups are formed. Some groups share a commitment to a category of products (sailing), to a specific brand (Harley-Davidson), or to a consumer activity (cultural tourism). These groups develop rituals and modes of communication which are defined on the basis of products and services. Group membership often requires adhering to a specific dress code and learning the symbols associated with it. Snowboarders, for example, do not dress in the same way as skiers, although in both cases their clothing must protect them from the cold.

DIFFERENT TYPES OF REFERENCE GROUP INFLUENCE

When we contrasted the studies of Asch and Venkatesan, we saw that the influence of reference groups can take different forms. We can distinguish three types of reference group influence: informational, comparative, and normative (Table 7.1).

Informational influence

In some situations, consumers seek information which will help them make better decisions. In these situations, groups which are perceived to have expertise can serve as a reference. For example, before purchasing an old table, a person might consult an expert in antique furniture. As indicated in Table 7.1, the consumer's objective is to acquire knowledge; the group's power lies in its expertise, and we say the consumer's behaviour is based on their acceptance or internalization of that expertise.

Table 7.1 The different types of influence exerted by reference groups

Social influence type	Goal orientation	Nature of influence source	Type of power	Behaviour
Informational	Knowledge	Credibility	Expertise	Internalization
Comparative	Self-concept	Similarity	Reference	Identification
Normative	External reward	Power	Coercion	Compliance

Source: Burnkrant and Cousineau (1975).

Comparative influence

Sometimes consumers use a reference group as a model, meaning they identify themselves with that group. For example, a consumer who perceives himself (and wishes to be perceived) as a devoted fan of heavy metal music will adopt the standard behaviours and attitudes of this group. In this case, his objective is to affirm his image of himself (his self-concept) through reference to a group perceived as being similar. The power of the group therefore resides in its capacity to serve as a reference, and the behaviour of the consumer is one of identification.

Normative influence

In other situations, reference groups have the power to force a consumer to adopt certain behaviours. For example, parents often decide what clothes their children will wear, what food they will eat, what toys they will have, how long they can be on social media? Parents have influence over their children because, among other things, they have the power to distribute rewards and punishments. Likewise, during a pandemic, cinephiles must follow the rules established by their favourite cinema if they wish to keep attending screenings in person. In this case, the consumer's goal is to obtain rewards or avoid punishments. The reference group is perceived as having a power of coercion and the consumer is required to comply.

INFLUENCERS

A concept which elicits great interest whenever one talks about social influence is that of *opinion leaders*. In the digital era, the word *influencer* is often used instead, but the two terms refer to the same type: people who have the power to influence others in their consumption habits. Influencers have a significant presence on social media; there are legions of people on YouTube, Instagram, and other platforms who seek to earn a living by presenting different types of products and helping consumers make the best choices. What links may exist between the influencer and the product brands they review is not always revealed. However, consumers are not so easily fooled—they know or suspect that influencers are occasionally or even regularly sponsored by the companies behind those brands. The companies rely on the fact that the information conveyed by an influencer is perceived to be more objective and therefore is more likely to have an impact on the behaviour of the public. Since influencers are frequently consulted sources of information and have a real influence on consumers, marketers seek to identify them and send them products for evaluation.

Influencers have special characteristics that distinguish them from ordinary consumers. First, these people have more knowledge than the average person about the products and services in question. And, unlike the recommendations made by commercial sources of information (e.g., advertising), their statements are perceived as being more objective. In principle, influencers will not hesitate to criticize a product which fails to meet their requirements and those of the consumers who follow or listen to them. This candour is necessary if they wish to be perceived as credible, continue to exert influence, and increase their power of attraction. But influencers must also preserve their relationships with their sponsors. As a result, they must straddle the fence between the interests of these two groups. For example, they may choose only to criticize a sponsor's product for things they know to be insignificant, or they may downplay the criticism in a personal way (e.g., "In my case it's not something I worry about").

Influencers are passionate people. They are continually on the lookout for information relevant to the products and services which interest them. They visit stores, surf the web, talk to salespeople and brand experts, attend trade fairs, read specialist books, and so on. In addition to influencing their followers in terms of their purchasing the products and services under review, they often also help consumers learn about their area of interest in general way. Because they are passionate and have a lot of experience, influencers do not hesitate to buy new products and perhaps promote them. They can generally be described as highly innovative people.

Another important characteristic of influencers is that, for the most part, they are specialized in a single field. Thus, an influencer for clothing brands will not automatically qualify as an influencer for automobiles. But opinion leadership can extend to related areas. For example, influencers for high-fidelity audio systems might also exert an influence on the musical choices of their followers.

CULTURE

In the previous sections of this chapter, we saw that a consumer's behaviour is partly shaped by the behaviour of other people. Thus, a consumer who aspires to belong to a group, whether real or imaginary, will be inclined to share the values of that group, subscribe to the same opinions, have the same interests, and adopt the same attitudes and behaviours. The schemata or mental representations that guide our interaction with the environment (see Chapter 3) are generally consistent with the groups we refer to, and different from the groups we dissociate from.

This vision of social influence is pertinent, regardless of the group to which consumers refer. When this group consists of members of an entire society, we can describe the social influence as the effect of culture. Since most people can generally be classified as members of a society (the French or the Chinese, for example), their individual schemata will necessarily be influenced by those mental representations which abound in that society. In the words of the famous anthropologist Edward B. Tylor (1832–1917), culture is "that complex whole which includes knowledge, belief, art, law, morals, custom, and any other capabilities and habits acquired by man as a member of society" (Tylor, 1871, p. 1). More simply, we can say that culture corresponds to the schemata we share with the members of the society we refer to. As we saw in Chapter 4, culture is learned through the process of socialization. Agents of socialization—such as family, friends, schools, religious groups, and media sources—help individuals to develop the schemata which are specific to a given culture.

Since a society is a group, the concepts we have seen with respect to reference groups are equally relevant when it comes to culture. The influence of culture can therefore be informational in nature; for example, the society we belong to informs us, directly or indirectly, of our rights and freedoms and of our duties. Its influence can also be comparative; for example, we may identify ourselves with our country by proudly supporting the athletes who represent us at the Olympic Games. A third type is the normative; it applies to the laws and regulations which ensure the proper functioning of society.

There is, however, a fundamental characteristic of culture that distinguishes it from reference groups: its effects are not directly visible, because culture is all-pervasive. Although our beliefs, opinions, interests, attitudes, and behaviours are influenced by culture, we are not aware of it. To discern the effects of culture, one has to take a comparative approach, which means to compare and contrast the behaviour of people who are members of different societies.

One such approach, that of the psychologist Geert Hofstede (1928–2020), has had a great deal of influence on social science and marketing researchers who investigate the effects of culture. Basing his studies on the inhabitants of many different countries (see Hofstede, 1984), he concluded there are four fundamental cultural dimensions by which societies can be contrasted: (1) power distance, or the degree to which hierarchical differences in social status are internalized by members of the society; (2) individualism, or the degree to which the actions of members of a society are based on the person rather than the group; (3) uncertainty avoidance, or the degree to which ambiguity is not tolerable; and (4) masculinity, or the degree to which members of a society display masculine values (such as performance, competition, heroism).[1] In his classic book *Culture's Consequences* (1984), Hofstede uses survey results from around 40 different countries to produce scores (ranging from 0 to 100) in each of these dimensions; the higher the score, the more the value is present. For example, the scores for five countries are shown in Table 7.2: Austria, Canada, Colombia, Italy, and Japan.

Table 7.2 The position of five countries according to the cultural dimensions of Hofstede

Country	Power distance	Individualism	Uncertainty avoidance	Masculinity
Austria	11	55	70	79
Canada	39	80	48	52
Colombia	67	13	80	64
Italy	50	76	75	70
Japan	54	46	92	95

Source: Hofstede (1984).

Looking at the five countries featured in this table, we can see that Austria and Canada are societies where differences in status between people (power distances) are less internalized; Canada and Italy are more individualistic societies; Canada is a society where uncertainty is more tolerated; and, last, masculine values are most present in Japan than elsewhere. Armed with a knowledge of these differences, one can make predictions regarding the multiple variables which characterize consumers and their behaviour. For example, one could form a hypothesis that consumers of art and cultural products who live in societies with a low degree of uncertainty avoidance (i.e., with a greater tolerance of uncertainty) will be more likely to consume new and diverse products. By the same token, consumers who live in more individualistic societies might be more likely to seek arts and culture products associated with personal satisfaction (e.g., reading novels, virtual museum visits) than with collective satisfaction (e.g., participation in a festival). Such statements are highly speculative, of course, and need to be verified by rigorous research. The essential lesson, however, is that a knowledge of a society's position with respect to basic cultural dimensions such as those proposed by Hofstede (1984) can partly explain how the members of that society behave as consumers.

SUBCULTURES

A group, as we have seen, is formed by people who share common values, which are the schemata distinguishing them from members of other groups. Thus, a society is a group whose members are defined by a shared culture—what Hofstede (1984)

calls *cultural dimensions*—which imposes a particular stamp upon each of its members. A culture develops and affirms itself over the centuries; it reflects the aggregate of a great number of events which have shaped and continue to shape it. Anyone who visits a foreign country quickly discovers that its native inhabitants share many of the characteristics or behavioural aspects one generally associates with their culture.

But one should avoid believing that a society is a cultural monolith. In the United States, for example, cultural differences (values, ways of thinking, beliefs, behavioural orientations, etc.) emerge in stark relief when one travels from one state to another. One can therefore surmise that the inhabitants of a certain place (a state, a region) within the larger society may develop a culture of their own; the groups which are formed in this way are called subcultures.

Other dimensions besides where one lives are likely to cause cultural differences that lead to the formation of subcultures. Among the most important dimensions are ethnicity (e.g., Canadians of Haitian descent), age (e.g., seniors), social class (e.g., blue collars), sexual orientation (e.g., gay men), and consumption (e.g., skilled surfers—a type of consumer tribe). When people share similar values, schemata, beliefs, and the like—that is, when they position themselves in a comparable way within pertinent cultural dimensions—they may form a subculture. In consequence, a very large number of possible subcultures exist.

REFERENCE GROUPS, CULTURE, AND SUBCULTURES IN THE FIELD OF ARTS AND CULTURE

Reference groups

Earlier we saw that in the marketing of arts and culture, the two main sources of influence upon someone who is planning their night out, and considering a venue to attend, are media reviews and peer information (word-of-mouth—WOM). We have also seen that the assessment made by experts usually matches the one made by non-experts (fans).

Let us return to the concept of WOM. Two types can be distinguished. One is self-oriented. It consists of a person talking about themselves to their extended reference group by posting information about themselves on social networks. The second type is externally oriented WOM, which conveys a person's taste or distaste for a cultural product such as a film, concert, or evening show.

Self-oriented WOM seeks to present one's personality and tastes to a public audience that resembles us (Saenger et al., 2013). The person expresses their preferences in arts and culture (e.g., music, films, exhibitions) and various elements that make up their experiential world (e.g., travel, cosmetics, parties with friends). Externally oriented WOM seeks to inform one's reference group with an appreciation or criticism of a product or experience (film, theatre, festival, restaurant); thus, a person will not speak of themselves but produce the equivalent of a review criticizing an object which exists (or event which occurs) outside of them.

For cultural organizations, it is important that WOM be positive, as it can have a direct effect on sales. Positive WOM can generate an increase in the number of viewers, which can lead to more WOM and so on (Duan et al., 2008). WOM is therefore an important variable for a cultural organization, even though it has no control over it.

It should be noted that this way of communicating with the reference group affects the central product (the work or artistic experience) differently than the peripheral products of an experience (e.g., changing rooms, coffee, hospitality, parking). Studies have shown that, in general, consumers present both the positive and the negative sides of the experiences they have. With regard to peripheral elements, however, they tend to share their views more often when the experience has been negative (Waller and Waller, 2019; Zanibellato et al., 2018). One social network member's negative opinion about a work of art may be offset by another member's positive opinion, but in cases where only the negative aspects of an experience are mentioned, as normally occurs for the peripheral elements, the unfavourable opinion will prevail. This affirms, once again, an important principle for marketers in arts and culture institutions: the value of enhancing the experiential components (the reception area, the seats, the staff) which surround the main product they offer (the play, the concert, the performance).

Culture and subcultures

Culture

A few researchers have trained their lens on how consumers perceive entertainment products which originate from cultures other than their own. For example, a comparative study by d'Astous et al. (2008) used survey data collected from five countries (Australia, Canada, the United States, Italy, and Switzerland) to measure and contrast the perceived image of 16 countries (France, the United States, Italy, China, Switzerland, Mexico, Belgium, Canada, Morocco, Austria, South Korea, England, Russia, Japan, Brazil, and Australia) in relation to 9 different artistic and cultural products (theatre, opera, classical music, art museums, action and adventure films, novels, comics, ballet, and jazz music). The researchers discovered that the more familiar we are with a country, the more positively we view it and the more favourably we judge the artistic and cultural products which originate from it. Similarly, an openness to foreign cultures, a positive bias in relation to one's own culture, or physical proximity to a culture, all have a positive effect on how one judges their products (d'Astous et al., 2008).

Another comparative study was conducted among cinephiles in Austria, Canada, Colombia, and Italy (d'Astous et al., 2005). These countries were selected because they show marked difference in three of the four cultural dimensions established by Hofstede (1984), namely, power distance, uncertainty avoidance, and individualism. The results showed that Canadians appreciate a greater diversity of film genres than Austrians, Colombians, and Italians do (an effect of the lower degree of uncertainty avoidance in Canada). In the field of cinema, Canadians and Austrians are alike in being more susceptible than Colombians or Italians to social influence based on the expression of values.

Other studies of consumer perceptions of products from different cultures enrich our understanding of the effects of this variable. For example, Bose and Ponnam (2011) used India as the consumer country to study the phenomenon of cultural or cognitive distance from a country and its cultural products. They showed that the cultural product preferences of Indian consumers exhibit variance according to the country (or culture) of origin. For example, Indian consumers make a favourable association of the United States with films, music, and circus shows; of England mainly with films; and of Russia with music and dance, theatre, and circus shows. According to the researchers, these differences can be explained by language, (since Indians share the English language with the United States and England); by the fact that India is a former colony of England; and by the country's rapprochement with Russia in the post-independence era. By contrast, Indian consumers have no affinity with a country like Brazil, for example, which is far removed from them in both culture and language. Similar results were observed for the tourism industry (Ng et al., 2007). In their study of intentions by Australians to visit 11 different countries, the researchers noted that consumers want to visit New Zealand, the United States, England, and Singapore but are less inclined to visit Japan, Germany, or Indonesia. According to the researchers, this difference can be explained by the proximity of Australian culture to the cultures of the former group. They emphasize, however, that their results relate to a population's intentions. The desire to consume foreign cultural products or to visit more culturally distant countries is more present among consumers who demonstrate great openness to the world (Ng et al., 2007).

Subcultures

All the statistics from industrialized countries indicate that the majority of the customer base for sophisticated art is recruited from people with a university degree, whereas popular art attracts both those with a degree and those who are less well educated (Colbert et al., 2018).

The writings of the sociologist Pierre Bourdieu advanced the concept of *habitus*, a system of values specific to a society or a social class. The so-called upper class, for example, focuses on classical music, theatre, and art museums as a way of distinguishing itself from the average population, which prefers popular art. In a way, class-based habitus corresponds to a subculture.

Bourdieu conducted his analysis in the 1970s. Other researchers then enriched his analysis by proposing other concepts and analytical models. Peterson (1992), for example, proposed the concept of *cultural omnivore* as a better term for distinguishing the upper class from the rest of the population in terms of their habitus. Since more and more people hold university degrees (30%–40%, depending on the country), and interest in high art is therefore growing, Peterson (1992) proposed that the old category of "upper class" (whose members were distinct for their interest in scholarly or sophisticated art) was now distinguished by the variety of its cultural consumption—by its *cultural omnivorousness* for both sophisticated and popular art.

Another team of researchers (Holbrook et al., 2002) analysed the question and concluded that the portrait is more complex than it may appear. They identified three types of situation. The first, which they call *effacement*, occurs when certain things are liked by everyone—for example, when highly educated and less educated people share a liking for a certain kind of music or a certain type of artist (e.g., the Beatles). The second, the *omnivore* situation, is present when some people like everything while others limit themselves to a particular genre. This is consistent with the fact that highly educated people participate in activities related to both popular and sophisticated art, while less educated people are interested in popular forms alone. Last, the *distinction effect* exists when the consuming of a certain type of product is a distinctive characteristic of a particular group and serves to signal their difference from other groups.

Other researchers have proposed the concept of *authenticity* as a functional component of the distinction effect. In this case, the cultural elite is able to discern what is authentic in popular culture from what is not (Bartmanski and Woodward, 2013; Goulding and Derbaix, 2019; Strand, 2014). This group is better equipped to appreciate the naïve artefacts or paintings which have the marks of authenticity, unlike other products which may be intended for tourists, for example. It is interesting to note that the preference for a product of the "popular art" kind perceived as authentic is stronger when the person feels insecure about their own degree of authenticity, or if the producing artists themselves are categorized as authentic (Hahl et al., 2017).

Additionally, Goldberg et al. (2016) have proposed another way to enrich the concept of cultural omnivorousness, by including the concepts of *variety* and *atypicality* in cultural consumption. In studying consumers from the point of view of variety, we can identify those who consume products from a diverse range of cultural genres. In considering them from the point of view of atypicality, on the other hand, we can identify those who are willing to combine two different products. An example of the first case would be a subculture of fans who like divergent genres of music at the same time, such as opera and hard rock. This group straddles a symbolic border which purists on both sides would disdain to cross. Atypical consumption, on the other hand, occurs when two genres are merged. In 1968, for example, Wendy Carlos and Benjamin Folkman recorded an album merging classical compositions by Johann Sebastian Bach and the use of a synthesizer (Goldberg et al., 2016, p. 220). Their album, entitled *Switched-On Bach*, was not to everyone's taste. While many music lovers enjoyed this fusion of two genres, some purists dismissed it as artistic heresy. These examples show two different types of omnivore: the group of consumers who enjoy varying genres of music but consume them separately, and the group of consumers who enjoy hybrid forms and the atypical mixing of genres.

IMPLICATIONS FOR THE MARKETING OF ARTS AND CULTURE

When we approach the concepts of culture and subculture, we touch on one of the fundamental challenges of expanding the market for the sophisticated forms of art. First, we must recognize the phenomenon of identifying with a subculture (social class) and its impact on the consumption of cultural products. Since consumption allows a person to show their membership in a social group, it is difficult to make that person consume products which do not fulfil their need or aspiration. For example, someone who wants to show they belong to a higher social class will not "lower" themselves by openly consuming the popular cultural products favoured by other social classes. By contrast, a person who has not internalized the codes affording them access to an appreciation of sophisticated art—and may have grown up with the idea, implicit or explicit, that theatre "is not for us, it is for people who are educated or wealthy" (or worse, that "we should not try to be something we are not")—will not show any interest at all in sophisticated forms of art. It thus becomes difficult to persuade the person to buy a ticket for a play or a classical music concert, because not only will they see no benefits in doing so, they will also be spurred into confirming their already acquired mental representations (the schemata formed earlier in life) as appropriate. Hence arises the interest in socializing children into an appreciation of sophisticated art—especially those who do not come from families where art is a regular part of life (Colbert and Courchesne, 2012). Schools can play a decisive role in acculturation strategies of this type. A teacher's passion for music or theatre, or for works of art, can be passed on to young people who are still at an age when their mind and their taste can be developed more easily. Even though young people may naturally find other interests during their teenage years, they can return to sophisticated art forms later in life, as we saw in the discussion of classical music in Chapter 2. We have long known that, in addition to the influence of the school environment, the act of visiting a cultural venue (a performance hall, a museum, a theatre) in youth increases the likelihood that a person will return to it after they reach adulthood. All the cultural mediation experiences created by museums and performing arts companies—such as shows for children and teenagers, special evenings and awards for a concert or opera performance, summer camps, and the like—help to form the future audience, assuming of course that these experiences are positive. However, it is still possible to arouse someone's interest in sophisticated art after they have reached adulthood. Unfortunately, an adult's newly formed interest is often tied to the cultural interests of the spouse, so if the couple separates, the person may quickly lose that interest (Gainer, 1995).

We have seen that how consumers perceive products from a culture other than their own may inhibit or (conversely) encourage tourism, particularly cultural tourism, and likewise may inhibit the purchase of cultural products. From this we see how worthwhile it is for a given country to use cultural diplomacy to get closer to other countries. When artists or performing arts companies display or produce their work abroad, they help to forge a rapprochement between two countries by promoting a positive image of their domestic culture in people's minds. For example, young people in Western countries formed a greater general appreciation of South Korea and its culture after the "K-Pop" musical phenomenon swept around the world in the 2010s.

IMPLICATIONS FOR RESEARCH

Relatively few studies have examined the influence of reference groups in the field of arts and culture. New research studies should be undertaken to update our understanding of the reference groups to which cultural consumers compare themselves—particularly by exploring the hypothesis that the processes of influence function differently as the products and services change and as the consumer situations change. What do we know about the influence exerted by aspirational groups when a consumer is deciding whether to subscribe to a theatre's seasonal programme? When the cultural product is consumed in private (on the web, for example) rather than in a public setting (at a theatre or concert hall), does the nature of the influence change?

Studies which have examined the influence of film critics (e.g., d'Astous and Colbert, 2002) fall partly within the category of research on influencers. However, unlike film critics, who are often respected figures in the media world, the influencers we see on social media are ordinary people by definition—microcelebrities, perhaps, who are equipped with superior knowledge of the products and services they promote or disparage, but ordinary people nonetheless. As we have noted, consumers are quite aware that businesses regularly ask influencers to evaluate their products and services. We may therefore form a hypothesis that these consumers engage in analysis that goes beyond the strict content of the evaluations: for example, they may seek to learn whether these evaluations are favourably biased or whether negative product reviews are intentionally minimized to avoid damaging the brand too much. This research area is completely virgin territory in the marketing of arts and culture.

Further research is also needed for enhancing our understanding of how consumers from different cultures behave in relation to products and services in the arts. The cultural dimensions proposed by Hofstede (1984) provide a helpful theoretical basis for this type of comparative research, as several studies have shown (e.g., d'Astous et al., 2005). Such comparative studies are difficult because of the multiple constraints upon the collection of data (sampling and measurement equivalence, for example, pose a real challenge), but they represent a necessary condition if we are to expand this marketing discipline to a global scope and truly understand how cultural products and the arts are consumed around the world.

Note

1 Two additional dimensions appear in Hofstede's more recent writings: long-term orientation and indulgence. We shall not look at these concepts in the present chapter since the majority of studies in this field have used the four dimensions mentioned above. For more information, visit https://geerthofstede.com/culture-geert-hofstede-gert-jan-hofstede/6d-model-of-national-culture

REFERENCES

Asch, S. E. (1955), "Opinions and Social Pressure", *Scientific American*, 193 (5), 31–35.

Bartmanski, D. and I. Woodward (2013), "The Vinyl: The Analogue Medium in the Age of Digital Reproduction", *Journal of Consumer Culture*, 15 (1), 3–27.

Bose, S. and A. Ponnam, (2011), "Country of Origin Effect on Services: An Evaluation of Entertainment", *Managing Leisure*, 16 (2), 98–107.

Burnkrant, R. E. and A. Cousineau (1975), "Informational and Normative Social Influence in Buyer Behavior", *Journal of Consumer Research*, 2 (3), 206–215.

Colbert, F. and A. Courchesne (2012), "Critical Issues in the Marketing of Cultural Goods: The Decisive Influence of Cultural Transmission", *City, Culture and Society, 3 (4), 275–280.*

Colbert, F. et al. (2018), *Marketing Culture and the Arts*, 5th edition, Montreal: Carmelle and Rémi-Marcoux Chair in Arts Management, HEC Montréal.

d'Astous, A., A. Carù, O. Koll, and S. P. Sigué (2005), "Moviegoers' Use of Film Reviews in the Search for Information: A Multi-Country Study," *International Journal of Arts Management*, 7 (3), 32–45.

d'Astous, A. and F. Colbert (2002), "Moviegoers' Consultation of Critical Reviews: Psychological Antecedents and Consequences", *International Journal of Arts Management*, 5 (1), 24–35.

d'Astous, A., Z. Giraud Voss, F. Colbert, A. Carù, M. Caldwell, and F. Courvoisier (2008), "Product-Country Images in the Arts: A Multi-Country Study", *International Marketing Review*, 25 (4), 379–403.

Duan, W., B. Gu, and A. B. Whinston (2008), "The Dynamics of Online Word-Of-Mouth and Product Sales—An Empirical Investigation of the Movie Industry", *Journal of Retailing*, 84 (2), 233–242.

Gainer, B. (1995), "Rituals and Relationships: Interpersonal Influences on Shared Consumption", *Journal of Business Research*, 32, 253–260.

Goldberg, A., M. T. Hannan, and B. Kovács (2016), "What Does It Mean to Span Cultural Boundaries? Variety and Atypicality in Cultural Consumption", *American Sociological Review*, 81 (2), 215–241.

Goulding, C. and M. Derbaix (2019), "Consuming Material Authenticity in the Age of Digital Reproduction", *European Journal of Marketing*, 53 (3), 545–564.

Hahl, O., E. W. Zuckerman, and M. Kim (2017), "Why Elites Love Authentic Lowbrow Culture: Overcoming High-Status Denigration with Outsider Art", *American Sociological Review*, 82 (4), 828–856.

Hofstede, G. (1984), *Culture's Consequences*, Newbury Park, CA: Sage Publications.

Holbrook, M. B., M. J. Weiss, and J. Habich (2002), "Disentangling Effacement, Omnivore, and Distinction Effects on the Consumption of Cultural Activities: An Illustration", *Marketing Letters*, 13 (4), 345–357.

Jones, E. E. and H. B. Gerard (1967), *Foundations of Social Psychology*, New York, NY: John Wiley & Sons.

Ng, S. I., J. A. Lee, and G. N. Soutar (2007), "Tourists' Intention to Visit a Country: The Impact of Cultural Distance", *Tourism Management*, 28 (6), 1497–1506.

Peterson, R. A. (1992), "Understanding Audience Segmentation: From Elite and Mass to Omnivore and Univore", *Poetics*, 21, 243–258.

Saenger, C., V. Thomas, and J. Wiggins Johnson (2013), "Consumer Focused Self- Expression Word of Mouth: A New Scale and Its Role in Consumer Research", *Psychology & Marketing*, 30 (11), 959–970.

Strand, M. (2014), "Authenticity as a Form of Worth", *Journal for Cultural Research*, 18, (1), 60–77.

Tylor, E. B. (1871), *Primitive Culture*, London: John Murray Ltd.

Venkatesan, M. (1966), "Experimental Study of Consumer Behavior Conformity and Independence", *Journal of Marketing Research*, 3 (4), 384–387.

Waller, D. S. and H. J. Waller (2019), "An Analysis of Negative Reviews in Top Art Museums' Facebook Sites", *Museum Management and Curatorship*, 34 (3), 323–338.

Zanibellato, F., U. Rosin, and F. Casarin (2018), "How the Attributes of a Museum Experience Influence Electronic Word-of-Mouth Valence: An Analysis of Online Museum Reviews", *International Journal of Arts Management*, 21 (1), 76–90.

CONCLUSION
PART 5

Marketing culture and the arts

Chapter 8

In this concluding chapter, we aim to briefly discuss the relationship between marketing and the field of arts and culture. All through the preceding chapters, we have presented concepts and applications which seek to document the behaviour of arts and culture consumers for the sake of improving the performance of organizations working in this domain. Is it unethical to use this research knowledge about consumers to sell them artistic and cultural products? Is it manipulation? These are legitimate questions for arts and culture organizations—when they try, for example, to persuade prospective clients to buy a ticket or subscribe to a series of concerts. What answers can we propose? Are there any satisfactory answers to be found?

First, we believe it is important to distinguish between (1) wanting a person to buy something they do not need, (2) responding to a legitimate need or desire they may have, and (3) having something which is likely to benefit them, even if they initially do not want it.

Consider the following example. When scientists around the world state that humanity, in ecological terms, is "in a race to the bottom" because we neglect the planet, don't we have every reason to do everything we can to convince our fellow citizens to work together and make our societies carbon-neutral? Knowing the psychological mechanisms that make some people disbelieve in the phenomenon of climate change is, from this perspective, a definite advantage. If the goal is to persuade climate change deniers, or people who have doubts about the adverse effects of climate change or our responsibility for it, we shall be better

DOI: 10.4324/9780429263118-13

equipped to change their beliefs, attitudes, and behaviours if we understand what leads them to think the way they do. Is this not a worthy goal, even if the people whom we target are completely uninterested? This is not the same as getting someone to buy a product which is useless. Often, the things we initially regard as useless may bring us great satisfaction in the end.

For example, how can you convince a person that junk food is harmful to their health, when they experience pleasure and satisfaction from eating it? Repression serves no purpose; we must find compelling arguments. To do so, we first need to understand what leads this person to behave as they do. The mechanisms may be psychological (such as a problem of self-esteem) or social (a family or work environment that does not promote healthy eating, for example). Understanding how humans function is a definite advantage in designing an information campaign which seeks to bring about a change in attitude and behaviour. Arguments that are not based on valid reasoning and research will be useless because they will not change how consumers behave.

We are all consumers, and we generally need to be wary of anyone who is trying to get us to buy a product we do not need. In this regard, it must be borne in mind that the needs which a product seeks to meet are often psychological rather than strictly utilitarian. We eat sugar not because it is good for our health, but because it tastes good and brings us pleasure. Rational arguments may persuade some people to reduce their sugar consumption, whereas other people will not be susceptible to such arguments. This resistance may, for example, result from a psychological need which acts as a salient belief associated with their sugar consumption. To convince them, one must first identify this need, especially since the person will have an immediate price to pay (going without a favourite pleasure) for a benefit which will come in the long term (better health). The same is true of antismoking campaigns. Quitting smoking requires sustained effort and great willpower. Everyone who has gone through this process knows it is not easy. Suffering is immediate, while health gains are felt in the longer term. It is better, then, to use arguments which will bring immediate benefits, in addition to those which occur in the long run. Depicting the way other people see you, for example, is a pertinent type of information campaign to promote the short-term benefits of quitting smoking. If your reference group or your spouse finds your smoky odour disgusting, perhaps this argument will be more effective than one based strictly on the idea that smoking cigarettes is bad for your health.

What about those people whose job it is to convince the public to come and admire an artist's work? One thing is certain—we should not try to persuade people on the basis of false arguments, or they will never come back if they are disappointed. "Just common sense", you say? Yes, of course, but we still need to be aware of it. For example, many of us have trusted a film critic's rave review but then found ourselves leaving the cinema sorely disappointed by the quality of the film and saying to ourselves, "Never gonna trust him again!"

No artist wants to perform in front of an empty room. Everyone who works in the arts is naturally, and correctly, convinced that what they do is useful to society. On the other hand, not everyone outside of the arts field is going to agree. There are many different motivations for going (or not going) to the theatre. Some people simply have no desire for it; they are nonstarters as an audience. There are people who would like to attend theatre shows but cannot afford it. Others have the means but not the time. Last, there are tastes and preferences which influence the decision process. In short, you like something or you don't, and changing your tastes is not a simple operation even when you wish to do so. This is the stage where knowledge of the consumer becomes essential. One must know how to talk to each subgroup of potential consumers and to do so with convincing arguments but without trying to sell them what they do not wish to buy or what they will be unhappy to have bought. The fictional case we outlined in the first chapter (Takumi and the opera) provides a good example. Had it not been for his friend Frank, would he ever have attended an opera performance? Would advertising campaigns, however good, have persuaded him to buy a ticket? The answer is probably no. Sometimes a person's reluctance to engage in an activity will appear almost absurd to us, but the potential customer's feelings are real and cannot be dismissed. Not knowing how to dress for an evening at the opera house can be a sufficient condition to prevent a person from buying a ticket when that person is concerned about how they appear in public. If we identify this factor, it becomes a simple matter to state, in a targeted promotion, that you can dress as you want to for the opera—that you do not need to wear a bow tie or a dress. Any other argument may miss the target and lead to a waste of time and money.

Last, it is useful to recall that non-consumers of culture do not exist (Colbert et al., 2018). When one considers all those people who attend live performances, visit museums, go to the cinema, consume music and films on digital platforms, read novels, or watch soap operas on TV, one has to admit that virtually everyone, in one way or another, consumes artistic products of one kind or another.

It is true, on the other hand, that non-consumers of high art products do exist. Any person whose job involves cultural mediation will benefit from knowing the monetary, psychological, or sociological constraints which prevent a person from attending theatres or museums. To know the motivations, perceptions, attitudes, barriers, and past history of the audience you want to conquer—that is half the battle. For example, as Lauring et al. (2016) point out, people who do not visit museums think the venue and the art work it contains are, in a way, inaccessible to them, because they believe they lack the intellectual tools and the training necessary to understand them. They not only feel intimidated but also develop the sense that they are excluded from this type of experience. Strategies to convince these people to visit museums should therefore be based, at least in part, on mitigating these psychological barriers.

In closing our discussion, it is important to emphasize that marketing is a tool and not an end in itself. The people responsible for marketing in a cultural organization work to provide the company with the means necessary for the artist to realize their artistic dreams. The arts administrators work for those who produce and consume art—and for art itself.

REFERENCES

Colbert, F. et al. (2018), *Marketing Culture and the Arts*, 5th edition, Montréal: Carmelle and Rémi-Marcoux Chair in Arts Management, HEC Montréal.

Lauring, J. O., M. Pelowski, M. Forster, M. Gondan, M. Ptito, and R. Kupers (2016), "Well, If *They* Like It… Effects of Social Groups' Ratings and Price Information on the Appreciation of Art", *Psychology of Aesthetics, Creativity, and the Arts*, 10 (3), 344–359.

Scientific journals and training programmes related to arts and culture (A&C) marketing

Appendix 1

TRAINING PROGRAMMES

Many university programmes around the world focus on training future managers for work in arts administration and cultural organizations. Most of these programmes are found within associations whose mission is to advance knowledge and promote teaching methods that ensure sound training for their students. In North America, the main institution is the Association of Arts Administration Educators (AAAE). It includes roughly 50 master's programmes and nearly 100 bachelor's programmes. Most of these university programmes are instituted by specific academic departments (in art history, music, or theatre) or by the arts and humanities faculties themselves. A handful of these programmes are also found in business administration faculties. HEC Montréal, for example, offers two related degrees: *Master of Management of Cultural Enterprises* (MMCE) and *Master of Management in International Arts Management* (MMIAM). In Canada, we also find the Canadian Association of Arts Administration Educators (CAAAE), a small organization that gathers a dozen different programmes. In Europe, the European Network on Cultural Management and Policy (ENCATC) assembles nearly 150 training programmes in 39 countries. Just like the AAAE, this organization allows membership by a small number of programmes from other continents as well. Similar associations exist in South Korea and in China. Australia, Japan, India, and the various Latin American countries have also established training programmes in this field.

The first university programmes associated with arts management and cultural administration were established in the second half of the 1960s, in Europe and North America. After a slow progression up to the middle of the 1970s, there was a sharp increase around the world in the number of programmes available. An exception was mainland China, where arts administration training programmes were first established only in the early 2000s, when hundreds of such programmes were rapidly founded in university arts faculties and in conservatories all around the country.

SCIENTIFIC JOURNALS

The authors of this book have listed no fewer than 85 English-language journals that publish or have published articles on arts administration topics and issues. While some of these journals specialize in publishing the results of arts administration research, others are based in the field of marketing in general, and still others in related disciplines such as tourism, urban studies, sociology, or psychology. We present a list of these journals below, grouped into three categories. The list is not exhaustive, however, since there are sure to be articles in other journals, not listed here, that have escaped our attention.

1. Specialized journals
   Arts and the Market
   Consumption Markets & Culture
   International Journal of Arts Management
   International Journal of Nonprofit and Voluntary Sector Marketing
   Journal of Arts Management, Law, and Society
   Journal of Cultural Economics
   Journal of Popular Culture
   Museum Management and Curatorship
   Nonprofit and Voluntary Sector Quarterly
2. Journals on tourism, sociology, and psychology
   American Sociological Review
   American Journal of Sociology
   American Behavioral Scientist
   Annals of Tourism Research
   City, Culture and Society
   Cultural Sociology
   Cultural Studies of Science Education
   Cyberpsychology, Behavior, and Social Networking
   Empirical Studies of the Arts
   European Sociological Review
   International Journal of Contemporary Hospitality Management
   International Journal of Culture, Tourism, and Hospitality Research
   International Journal of Event and Festival Management
   International Journal of Event Management Research
   International Journal of Tourism Research
   International Journal of Urban Sciences
   Journal of Convention & Event Tourism
   Journal of Economic Psychology
   Journal of Global Fashion Marketing
   Journal of Research in Personality
   Journal of Vacation Marketing
   Leisure Studies
   Musicae Scientiae
   Music Perception
   Place Branding and Public Diplomacy
   Poetics
   Popular Music and Society
   Psychology of Music
   Psychology of Aesthetics, Creativity, and the Arts
   Reading Psychology

Scandinavian Journal of Hospitality and Tourism
Social Science Research
Sociology Compass
Tourism Management
Tourism Management Perspectives
Sociological Quarterly

3. Journals on marketing, administration, or management

Academia Revista Latinoamericana de Administración
Academy of Management Journal
Advances in Consumer Research
Australasian Marketing Journal
Business and Management Studies
Business Process Management Journal
British Journal of Management
Canadian Journal of Administrative Sciences
European Journal of Marketing
International Journal of Research in Marketing
Journal of the Academy of Marketing Science
Journal of Advertising Research
Journal of Business Research
Journal of Consumer Behaviour
Journal of Consumer Culture
Journal of Consumer Research
Journal of Marketing
Journal of Marketing Management
Journal of Marketing Research
Journal of Marketing Theory and Practice
Journal of Operations Management
Journal of Product & Brand Management
Journal of Retailing
Journal of Retailing and Consumer Services
Journal of Service Management
Journal of Strategic Marketing
Long Range Planning
Management Decision
Management Dynamics in the Knowledge Economy
Marketing Intelligence & Planning
Marketing Letters
Marketing Review
Organization Science
Psychology & Marketing
Service Industries Journal
Qualitative Market Research
Quantitative Marketing and Economics

Index

Note: **Bold** page numbers refer to tables and *italic* page numbers refer to figures.

Aaker, J. L. 20, 28
adaptation: of messages to market 26; of organizations 3
Ahn, K. 82, 84
Ajzen, I. 68, 73, 82, 85
Anderson, A. 20, 29
Andreasen, A. R. 58, 65
anthropomorphism 20
appropriation: of an art object 38; process of 79
arts marketing and ethics 127–130
Aschaffenburg, K. 59, 65
Asch, S. E. 105–107, 123
assimilation, process of 35
associative memory network *54*, 54–55, 57, 62, 73, 76
attitude: cognitive structure of an 69, *70*, **71**; components of an 69; definition of 68; one-dimensional perspective of 69, *69*; three-dimensional perspective of 69
authenticity 24–25, 119

Bagozzi, R. P. 74, 76, 84
Baker, J. 78, 84
Balloffet, P. 18, 28, 34, 46, 52, 55, 65, 69
Barret, M. 61, 65
Bar-Tal, A. 86
Bartmanski, D. 119, 123
Bearden, W. O. 95, 101
Beauregard, C. 43, 46
Belk, R. W. 58, 65
Bergel, M. 41, 46
Bergkvist, L. 65
Berthomier, N. 59, 66
Boerner, S. 96, 101
bollywood 44
Bonetti, L. 22, 28
Bonneville, A. 24, 28
Bose, S. 117, 123
Boujbel, L. 20, 28
Boulaire, C. 18, 28, 34, 46, 52, 55, 65, 69
Bourdieu, P. 57, 65, 118
Bourgeon-Renault, D. 13, 42, 47, 80, 84
Bower, G. H. 76, 83, 84
Bransford, J. D. 37, 46

Bridson, K. 78, 85
Brock, C. 41, 46
Brown, C. L. 45, 48
Burnkrant, R. E. 110, 123

Caldwell, M. 27, 28, 117, 123
Carlston, D. E. 54, 67
Carrillat, F. A. 39, 46
Carù, A. 27, 28, 38, 45, 46, 58, 65, 117, 123
Casarin, F. 116, 124
categorization 34–35; and attitude formation 72; basic level of 35
Cervone, D. 19, 28
Chan, E. K. 78, 84
Charland-Lallier, M. 59, 65
Chebat, J.-C. 34, 46
Choo, H. 82, 84
Christin, A. 60, 65
Cito, M. C. 82, 86
classical conditioning 49–51, *50*, 64
cognitive dissonance 91
Cohen, J. B. 47, 84
Colbert, F. 4, 6, 13, 24, 27, 28, 39, 40, 43, 46, 59, 65, 74, 79, 81, 84, 85, 94, 97, 101, 117, 118, 121–123, 130
Colletti, P. 42, 47
Congram, C. A. 84
consumption: experiential 79–80, 93; omnivorousness 119, 120
consumption experience *10*, 10–11, 62, 75, 79
consumption of arts and culture 7–9; activities of 7–8; definition of 7; explanation of 9; model of the 9–12
consumption vocabulary 45
contrast, process of 35
Cooper, J. 91, 101
co-production/co-creation 78
Costa, M. 22, 28
Costa, P. T. 18, 29
Courchesne, A. 121, 123
Courvoisier, F. 27, 28, 117, 123
Cousineau, A. 110, 123
Cova, B. 38, 43, 45, 47, 58, 65
Cova, V. 80, 86
Crutchfield, R. S. 34, 47

Cui, A. P. 41, 48
cultural diplomacy 121
cultural transmission 57–59
culture: comparative studies of 117–118; definition of 112; dimensions of 113–114, **114**
customer service 81
Czepiel, J. A. 84

Daghfous, N. 18, 28, 34, 46, 52, 55, 65, 69
Damen, M.-L. 59, 66
d'Andrade, E. 84
Dantas, D. C. 4, 13, 79, 84, 97, 101
d'Astous, A. 18, 20, 28, 34, 39, 46, 47, 52, 55, 65, 69, 74, 85, 94, 101, 117, 122, 123
d'Astous, E. 24, 28
Debenedetti, S. 63, 66, 79, 85
decision-making process 87–93, *88*; types of *98*, 98–99
decision rules 90
decisions: individual *versus* group 92; multiplicity of 92; rationalist character of 92–93; types of 92
Derbaix, C. 76, 85
Derbaix, M. 25, 28, 119, 124
Détrez, C. 59, 66
Deutsch, M. 95, 101
Duan, W. 116, 123
Dubois, B. 101
Dusseault, P. 96, 102

Ekinci, Y. 24, 28
elaborative processing 55, 65
emotions: definition of 74; dimensional approach of 75–76; Richins's typology of 75, **75**, 82
Escoffier, N. 96, 101
Etzel, M. J. 95, 101
Euzéby, F. 93, 102
Evans, J. 78, 85

Farrell, A. 46
Filiatrault, P. 34, 46
Fishbein, M. 68, 69, 73, 82, 85
formation of tastes in art 57
Forster, M. 130
Fraser, P. 40, 47
Friestad, M. 38, 47

Gaidis, W. C. 51, 67
Gainer, B. 60, 66, 79, 85, 95, 102, 121, 124
Gélinas-Chebat, C. 34, 46
Gerard, H. B. 95, 101
Gilovich, T. 90, 102
Giraud Voss, Z. 27, 28
Glennie, E. J. 61, 67
Goldberg, A. 120, 124

Goldberg, L. R. 22, 29
Gombault, A. 42, 47, 80, 84
Gondan, M. 130
Gopinath, M. 74, 76, 84
Goulding, C. 25, 28, 119, 124
Graeff, T. R. 21, 28
Greenberg, D. M. 22, 28
Griffin, D. 90, 102
Gu, B. 116, 123

Haanstra, F. 59, 66
Habich, J. 119, 124
habitus 118
Hahl, O. 25, 28, 119, 124
Hannan, M. T. 120, 124
Haugtvedt, C. P. 84, 85
Hausmann, A. 59, 66
Ha, Y.-W. 45, 47
Herr, P. M. 84, 85
hierarchical distance 113
Hirschman, E. C. 93, 102
Hoch, S. J. 45, 47, 48
Hofstede, G. 113–114, 117, 124
Holbrook, M. B. 60, 66, 93, 102, 119, 124
Hosany, S. 24, 28
Howard, J. A. 92, 102
Hume, M. 97, 102

implications for research: of attitudes and affective states 81–84; of the concept of learning 63–65; of the concept of perception 45–46; of the concepts of culture and subculture 122–123; of the concepts of personality and self-concept 27–28; of the decision-making process 100–101
implications for arts marketing: of attitudes and affective states 81; of the concept of learning 62–63; of the concept of perception 44–45; of the concepts of culture and subculture 120–122; of the concepts of personality and self-concept 26; of the decision-making process 98–100
incorrect inferences 43–44
individualism 113
influencers 110–112
information processing 52–55
information search 89–90, **90**; from critical reviews 95
instrumental conditioning 51–52
intangibility of arts and culture products 40
interpretation 36–38
Isen, A. M. 77, 84, 85

Johnson, M. D. 12, 91
Johnson, M. K. 37, 46

Kahn, B. 84, 85
Kahneman, D. 90, 102
Kamau, E. 45, 46
Kardes, F. R. 84, 85
Kassarjian, H. H. 19, 29
Kerrigan, F. 40, 47
Kim, M. 25, 28, 119, 124
Koll, O. 117, 123
Kosinski, M. 22, 28
Kovács, B. 120, 124
Kraaykamp, G. 59, 66
Kracman, K. 57, 66
Krech, D. 34, 47
Kruglansky, A. 86
Kupers, R. 130

Laroche, M. 40, 47
Lauring, J. O. 130
learning: from the behaviourist perspective 49–52; from the cognitive perspective 52, 52–55; of culture 112; gendered 60–61; from the socialization perspective 55–57
Lee, J. A. 118, 124
Lee, N. 46
Le Gall-Ely, M. 42, 47, 80, 84
Lévesque, M. 20, 28
Levitin, D. J. 22, 28
Lichtlé, M.-C. 52, 66
Lloyd, B. B. 47
Lowrey, T. M. 101
loyalty: of art consumers and culture 81, 97; brand 52
Lubbers, M. 6, 59

Maas, I. 59, 65
Malouff, J. M. 23, 29
market segments 26, 99
Martinez, C. 93, 102
masculinity 113
Mason, D. D. M. 43, 47
Matusitz, J. 44, 47
McCarthy, C. 43, 47
McKelvey, B. 96, 101
McRae, R. R. 18, 29
Mehrabian, A. 75, 85
memory: episodic 53; long-term 53; semantic 53; short-term 53
Mercklé, P. 59, 66
Meuleman, R. 59, 66
Michael. J. 25, 29
Miesen, H. W. J. M. 82, 85
Minkiewicz J. 78, 85
Minor, M. S. 76, 86
Monteiro, B. L. 22, 28

Montpetit, D. 74, 84
mood 76–77, 84
Moschis, G. P. 55, 66
multi-attribute model: critical assessment of the 72–73; extension of the 73–74; measurement of the components of the 70–71; strategic implications of the 72
Mulyanegara, R. C. 20, 29
Myers-Briggs 18

Nagel, I. 59, 66
need: ethics and 127–128; recognizing a 88–89
negative review 34
Neisser, U. 37, 45, 47, 54, 66
Nepomuceno, M. V. 40, 47
Ng, S. I. 118, 124
Nobert, V. 94, 101
nonparticipants/non-consumers 61, 130
nostalgia 60
Nyer, P. U. 74, 76, 84

Obaidalahe, Z. 79, 81, 85, 97, 102
Octobre, S. 59, 66
Oliver, R. L. 52, 66
Onkvisit, S. 29
opera 4–7
Ouellet, J.-F. 24, 27, 29
Özbilgin, M. 40, 47

pandemic 3
Parmentier, M.-A. 39, 46, 65
Payano, P. 44, 47
Pelowski, M. 130
perception: automatic 33–34; of causes 38; as a linear process 33; of price 41–42; of quality 42–43; of risk 40; and satisfaction 41; selective 33–34; voluntary or involuntary 33
perceptual cycle 37, 37–38, 45, 54
perceptual organization 34–36
personality: of consumption objects 20; definition of 18; dimensions of 18; of festivals 24; five-factor theory 19; marketing approaches to 19–20; and musical tastes 22–24; of performance halls 24; psychology research on 18–19; and reading preferences 23–24
Pervin, L. A. 19
Peterson, R. A. 119, 124
Petr, C. 42, 47, 80, 84
Petrick, J. F. 82, 84
Pham, M. T. 84
Plichon, V. 52, 66
Ponnam, A. 117, 123
post-decision processes 91
Potter, J. 24, 28

Preece, S. B. 96, 102
preferences: in music 22–23; in reading 23–24
Ptito, M. 130

Rajaobelina, L. 96, 102
Ravanas, P. 42, 47
reference groups: definition of 107; Solomon Asch's studies on 105–106; types of 108; types of influence of 109–110, **110**
reinforcement 51
relational/transactional consumer 97
Rempel, J. K. 73, 86
Rentfrow, P. J. 22–24, 28, 29
Renz, S. 96, 101
Ricard, L. 96, 102
Richard, M.-O. 40, 47
Richins, M. L. 75, 76, 82, 86
risk: economic 40; performance 40; psychological 40; reduction of 45; security 40
Roedder John, D. 56, 66
Rosch, E. 35, 47
Rosin, U. 116, 124
Rothschild, M. L. 51, 67
Russell, J. A. 75, 85

Saenger, C. 116, 124
Salerno, F. 79, 81, 85, 97, 102
satisfaction 91; of consumers of art and culture 97
Savard, M.-A. 24, 27, 29
Schafer, T. 22, 29
schema: of events 37; and memory network 54–55; of people 37; of places 37; as a structure for expectations 37–38
Schindler, R. M. 60, 66
Schmutz, V. 61, 67
Schutte, N. S. 23, 29
scientific journals 4, 22
Sedlmeier, P. 22, 29
self-concept 21–22, 24–26; consumption and 21–22; and consumption of arts and culture 26; definition of 21
Shanahan, J. 84
shaping 51, 62, 64
Shaw, J. 29
Sheth, J. N. 92, 102
Shrum, L. J. 101
Sigué, S. P. 117, 123
Sirgy, M. J. 21, 29
social environment 11–12, 79
social influence: comparative 110; informational 109–110; normative 110
socialization: of consumers 55–57; and the role of school 54; by sex 60–61; and the social media 59

socialization agents 57
Solomon, M. R. 33, 47
Song, C. 96, 102
Soscia, I. 82, 86
Soutar, G. N. 118, 124
spokesman 50, 64
sponsorship 39, 64
spreading activation 54–55, 62, 83
Srull, T. K. 85
Stearns, E. 61, 67
Stevenson, D. 61, 67
Stillwell, D. J. 22, 28
stimulus generalization 50–51
St-James, Y. 4, 13
Strand, M. 119, 124
structural and motivational factors 34
Stuckey, A. 7, 13
subcultures 114–115, 118–120; according to consumption 115; according to social class 115; by age 115; by sexual orientation 115

Tanford, S. 41, 47
theory: Big Five Personality Test 18; self-image congruence 21–22
theory of reasoned action 73, 74
Thomas, V. 116, 124
Touil, N. 39, 47, 94, 101
trendiness 24
Trivedi, D. 96, 102
Troilo, G. 82, 86
Tsarenko, Y. 20, 29
Tylor, E. B. 112, 124

uncertainty avoidance 12, 113
Urbain, C. 42, 47, 80, 84
Uysal, M. 23, 28

Valley, L. 43, 46
value (of a product or an experience) 41, 80
Vanhuele, M. 101
Vanisky, A. 34, 46
Venkatesan, M. 106, 107, 124
Ver, M. 59, 66
Voss, Z. G. 43, 47, 80, 86, 117, 123

Waller, D. S. 116, 124
Waller, H. J. 116, 124
Wang, Y. J. 76, 86
Weiss, M. J. 119, 124
West, P. M. 45, 48
Whinston, A. B. 116, 123
Wiggins, J. 41, 48, 96, 102
Wiggins Johnson, J. 116, 124
Wolf, T. 60, 67
Woodward, I. 19, 123
word-of-mouth 96, 115–116

Wright, P. L. 38, 47
Wu, S.-I. 41, 48
Wyer, R. S., Jr. 54, 67, 85

Xu, M. K. 24, 28

Yung, S. 41, 47

Zanibellato, F. 116, 124
Zanna, M. P. 73, 86
Zeithaml, V. 41, 48
Zhou, K. Q. 65
Zilca, R. 22, 29
Zimprich, D. 60, 67
Zuckerman, E. W. 25, 28, 119, 124